Needlework Animals

ELIZABETH BRADLEY

Needlework Animals

With over 25 Original Charted Designs

Trafalgar Square Publishing

First published in the United States of America in 1996 by Trafalgar Square Publishing,
North Pomfret, Vermont 05053

Color Separations by Colorlito, Rigogliosi, Milan
Printed in Italy by Officine Grafiche De Agostini - Novara 1996

1 3 5 7 9 10 8 6 4 2

Text and charts copyright © Elizabeth Bradley 1996
Photography copyright © Ebury Press 1996

Elizabeth Bradley has asserted her right under the Copyright Designs and Patents
Act, 1988, to be identified as the author of this work.

ISBN 1-57076-042-X
Library of Congress Catalog Card Number 95-61721

Editor: Emma Callery
Design: Janet James
Photographer: Nadia Mackenzie
Stylist: Elizabeth Bradley
Collages: Elizabeth Bradley

This book is for the Narkiewicz family, for Karen my indispensable and
invaluable assistant and her four sons, Adam, Marek, Alex and Joe, who checked all the
charts. With their help it has been a pleasure to write.

My thanks to Nadia Mackenzie for her wonderful photographs that introduce each chapter.

To Emma for editing it, to Janet for designing it, to Colette for checking the facts and
to Ebury for publishing it.

My thanks also to Mandy and all those kind stitchers who worked the models and counted
the wool. This book is very much a joint effort, impossible to undertake without all of your help.

*PREVIOUS PAGE: Collage: large flowers like these roses and
peonies provide food and shelter for a wide variety of insects.*

CONTENTS

Introduction

This is a book about some of the animals that share the planet Earth with us. It has been interesting to research and write, and it has also taken me pleasantly back to a three year period in my life when I studied for a degree in Zoology and Marine Zoology at Bangor University. I was rather surprised and pleased to discover how much I remembered; once learned, the overall organization of the animal kingdom and the general principles of evolution and ecology, are apparently never forgotten.

I have to admit at this stage, that though I like animals and find many of them both beautiful and interesting, I am not a dedicated natural historian. I am afraid that I do not spend most of my free time observing and studying animals out in the field nor am I a fanatical or even a very knowledgeable bird watcher. On the other hand, living where we do, only a few yards away from the Menai Straits, it would be difficult not to marvel at the panorama of bird life, weather and light laid out before me.

Our house is three storeys high and our bedroom is at the top. Drinking that first, essential cup of early morning coffee in bed, I am charmed each day by the ever changing view over the sea to the mountains of Snowdonia. Gulls often hover really close to the window, clouds of dunlin and flocks of curlews and oyster catchers forage at the water's edge, with maybe a couple of herons and our resident swan family nearby. Just a few miles away down the Straits at Puffin Island, grey seals breed on the rocks and the remaining puffins nest in holes on the cliffs.

The words 'remaining' or 'disappearing' or 'lost for ever' seem to be the rather sad refrain to any ode to nature written today. How much to dwell on the disappearance of species was one of the quandaries of this book. One cannot, of course, ignore the facts but I decided that I would try to take an optimistic approach overall and concentrate on the wonder and fascination of what is still here rather than mourn too much what is already gone. Some animal populations are actually on the increase, whales are watched rather than slaughtered *en masse* and seagulls, pigeons and rabbits are becoming a positive nuisance.

Rather than feature a succession of isolated and unrelated projects I have organized the book into a cohesive whole by grouping the various topics into chapters. Chapter one is a world view, literally a needlework carpet-sized animal atlas showing the distribution of a rather eccentric collection of animals. Recently, two Japanese visitors came to my studio and I showed them the atlas. Understandably they immediately looked for Japan and were rather disappointed to see their country represented by a starry flounder and a yellow fin tuna. In the same way, the British might be rather surprised to see a wildcat as the only animal inhabitant of Great Britain – I ask you to bear with me, read the relevant chapter and try to be tolerant if you feel that your national wildlife has not been fairly represented.

Chapters two, three and four feature animals of the air, water and land respectively. The tawny owl fire screen, the sperm whale bath mat and the mackerel glasses case should all be useful items and there are lots of ideas for cushions and small rugs.

Chapter five is a result of my early training. Any student of zoology learns about ecology and I have wanted to try to design some reasonably accurate habitat charts for years. So here they are and I hope you enjoy working them. They might appear complicated but they are considerably easier to work than they look.

Chapter six, Animals and Man, could have featured all sorts of creatures as man influences the lives of many of the species here on the Earth with us. In the end, I decided to limit myself to some of the domestic animals whose physical appearances have actually been changed by man. Cats, pigs and chickens could all survive quite well in the wild in spite of any alterations, but I am not sure about some of the more extreme dog breeds.

Chapter seven is perhaps my favourite – the little charts were such fun to paint and are so bright and cheerful when combined into a carpet. Because this book will be

published in France and Italy as well as in English-speaking countries, the alphabet works in French and Italian too. As a result, some of the animals are perhaps not the most obvious and traditional choice. Instead of D for dog or donkey or duck, for example, I have painted D for dorado which is a species of fish. Looking at it positively, at least children might learn to spell the names of some quite unusual animals.

The last section deals with materials and methods. The information there is very similar to that in my first two books *Decorative Victorian Needlework* and *Needlework Antique Flowers* but is worth reading, even if it is just to refresh your memory.

You will notice that most of the animals in this book have been given their Latin as well as their common names. Please ignore these names with my blessing if you wish, I put them in because I thought that they might be useful. Like the Latin names of plants and flowers, they are essential for identifying exactly which species is being discussed; common names can vary so much from country to country and even from one part of a country to another. Also, several animals often share the same common name even though they are actually different species living in slightly dissimilar ways and places. For instance, there are three species of golden mole rather than just one, and the one featured at the bottom of South Africa on the Animal Atlas is the giant golden mole, *Chrysospalax trevelyani*; not the Hottentot or Cape varieties which have different Latin names. So what!, you may feel, but someone, somewhere, might want to know.

The last two points that I would like to mention are questions of style, the first of illustration and the second of chart design. This book has been embellished or illustrated with a mixture of the usual charts and photographs but also, and more unusually, with a series of collage pictures. Making collages is fun to do and is a very popular pastime. The artform can be used to decorate almost anything from a print room to a picture frame, or as in this case, a book. The examples in this book were made to complement the designs and they have been interspersed among the photographs to add variety and visual interest. The needlework charts also vary in style. Some designs in the book are painted in the elaborate Victorian mode, others are much more naive, and the rest are somewhere in between. I enjoyed painting all three types of chart and hope you enjoy working them. I have tried to provide something for everyone, even for readers who really only like to stitch flowers – the Pig Pillow is for them.

RIGHT: The Tawny Owl. The project is featured on pages 36-9.

CHAPTER ONE

Animal Atlas

Animal Atlas Carpet

This animal atlas carpet is one of the most ambitious projects in this book. It is interesting to work and impressive and unusual when finished. Apart from its decorative value as a carpet or wall hanging, it could be both educational and fun for children – they might use it as a play rug. Plastic animals, small toy boats and planes could be moved around from one continent to another, just as my son used to push small cars around on one of those printed mats that show road networks.

Although it may seem as if there are an awful lot of animals crowded onto this carpet, there are in fact only a tiny fraction of those that could be featured. There are more than a million kinds of animal living on Earth today and we know that there are many more species still to be discovered in the future. This vast number of creatures has had to be divided or classified into six major groups to make it easier to study. The largest and most diverse group is the invertebrates (or animals without a backbone) and this includes insects, shellfish, corals, spiders and worms as well as many microscopic single-celled animals like amoebae. The other five groups all have backbones and are the amphibians, birds,

PREVIOUS PAGE: The Animal Atlas carpet being used as a play mat. Mixed herds of plastic animals are moving in from all sides to colonize the green land masses.

fish, reptiles and mammals. Most of the animals on this carpet are mammals although there are some fish, birds and reptiles and a few invertebrates like the octopus.

Mammals were the last to evolve, they are warm blooded animals with backbones and most of them are hairy and have four legs. Young are born after a period of development or gestation in the womb and are fed on milk produced from mammary glands. There are about 4,000 species of mammals alive today and they have evolved and adapted so as to be able to live in most types of habitats and conditions present on our planet. Whales, dolphins and seals live in the sea while otters, beavers and water rats have evolved to live in fresh water. On land, mammals such as moles, badgers and rabbits burrow underground, others graze on grassy plains or live high in trees. A few, like bats, are even able to fly. Some mammals are total vegetarians, some are carnivores eating only meat while others are omnivores, like man and bears, eating vegetation as well as other animals.

This needlework atlas gives some indication of the astonishing diversity of animals that are spread across the globe. The limited space available on the green land masses of the carpet meant that only a relatively few species could be shown on them. The chosen ones are a mixture of best loved and rather spectacular mammals such as elephants, reindeer, polar bears and tigers and the rarer – but often very interesting – animals that tend to inhabit specific corners of the world.

Some of the most fascinating animals on

Earth live in only one place or isolated group of islands so their hold on survival is rather tenuous; if their very restricted habitat is destroyed then they become extinct. For instance, one collection of rare animals including the manatee, Florida panther and roseate spoonbill are found only in the subtropical region in Florida known as the Everglades. This area is also in demand as a human playground which poses a threat to its animal inhabitants.

Most of the animals shown on the carpet have distinctive shapes and markings that make them easy to recognize from the small and simple charts. A lion or camel is easy to identify from its basic outline, whereas other mammals like rats or shrews look pretty similar the world over; the small differences between the species are too minimal to show clearly. Creatures that live in the sea are less visible but almost as diverse as those that live on land. Some are specific to a particular area but many range over large areas of the world's seas and oceans. Whales are probably the most magnificent of all aquatic animals and several species are shown on the carpet along with a few sharks and other fish.

Working the Animal Atlas carpet

The finished Animal Atlas carpet, including the border, measures 51.8 ins (131.5 cms) by 34.5 ins (87.5 cms). Although this a large piece to handle it is best made in one piece rather than in several sections which would need to be joined together later. Our Blue Line Canvas is 39 ins (1 m) wide so this carpet will not fit across it and can only be worked with the longer edge running parallel to the selvedge.

Pieces of needlework come out a better shape if the stitches are worked across the canvas from selvedge to selvedge so it is best to work this piece on its side. Start at the

bottom left-hand corner of chart four on page 18 and work across to the top left-hand corner of chart one opposite. Then work upwards through charts five and two on pages 19 and 16 and finally charts six and three on pages 20 and 17 until it is finished. The border should be treated as an integral part of the carpet and worked at the same time as the atlas.

For instructions on finishing and edging a carpet, please see page 113. This can be done in the same colour wool as the last two rows of the border, green (J11), or in any other colour of your choice.

The quantities listed below are the numbers of yards of Elizabeth Bradley wool needed to stitch a carpet and border measuring 518 stitches by 345 stitches on 10 mesh interlock canvas using cross stitch.

Colours used: 34

Number on chart key	Elizabeth Bradley wool colour	Quantity (yards)
1	B3	15
2	B11	79
3	C4	11
4	C5	75
5	C6	59
6	C7	100
7	D3	11
8	E1	18
9	E2	14
10	E3	22
11	E4	35
12	E5	18
13	E8	22
14	E9	15
15	F1	142
16	F3	66
17	F4	21
18	F6	15
19	F8	23
20	F9	18
21	F11	27
22	G4	18
23	G10	84
24	H2	75
25	H3	59
26	H5	59
27	H7	21
28	I1	11
29	I2	14
30	J6	351
31	J10	85
32	K10	9
33	L1	1250
34	L11	338

These quantities do not include wool for finishing and edging the carpet.

This line indicates the outer edges of the Animal Atlas charts

Central portion of the Animal Atlas carpet

Finishing the carpet as described on page 113 will make it two rows bigger all around than is shown on this chart

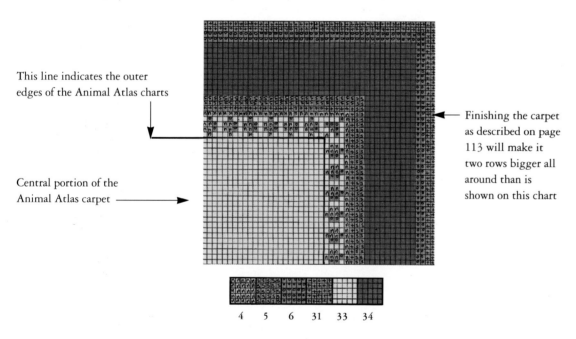

4   5   6   31   33   34

ABOVE: The chart for the border of the Animal Atlas carpet. For an indication of how this border fits onto the edge of the Animal Atlas carpet, please see Chart 3 on page 17. Please note that white snow instead of pale blue sea has been worked inside the border in Antarctica.

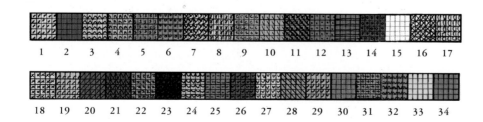

1   2   3   4   5   6   7   8   9   10   11   12   13   14   15   16   17

18   19   20   21   22   23   24   25   26   27   28   29   30   31   32   33   34

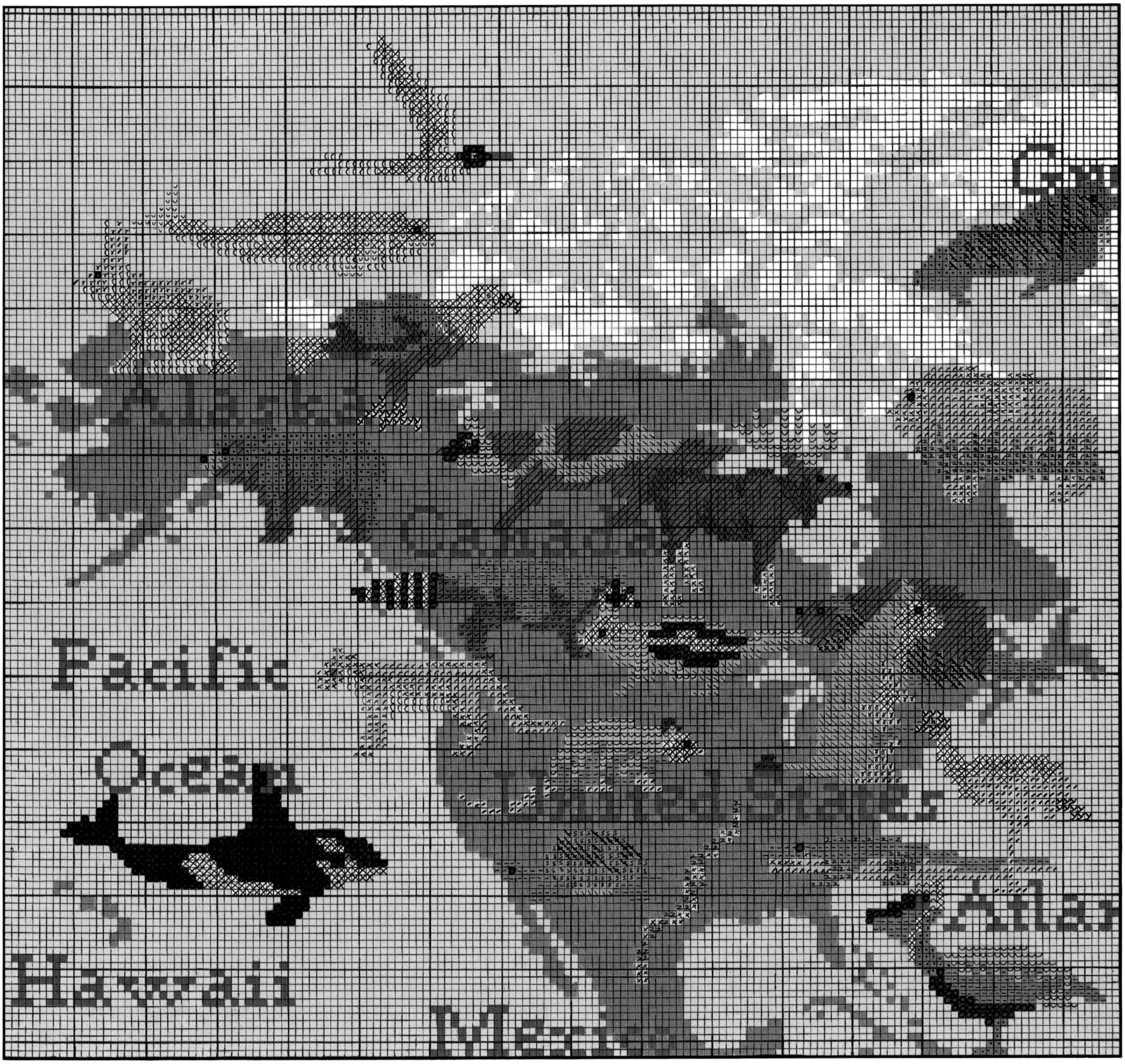

JOIN TO CHART 2

JOIN TO CHART 4

CHART 1 Contents: ARCTIC OCEAN Arctic Tern *Sterna paradisaea* Beluga Whale *Delphinapterus leucas*
GREENLAND Walrus *Odobenus rosmarus* ALASKA Arctic Hare *Lepus arcticus* Bald Eagle *Haliaeetus Leucocephalus* CANADA Grizzly Bear *Ursus arctos horribilis*
Wolverine *Gulo gulo* Raccoon *Procyon lotor* Moose *Alces alces* Musk Ox *Ovibos moschatus* Beaver *Castor canadensis* UNITED STATES AND MEXICO Mountain Lion
Felis concolor Chipmunk *Eutamias minimus* Opossum *Didelphis virginiana* Prairie Dog *Cynomys ludovicianus* Desert Tortoise *Gopherus agassizi* American Alligator *Alligator*
mississippiensis Roseate Spoonbill *Ajaia ajaia* Rattlesnake *Crotalus atrox* Brown Pelican *Pelecanus occidentalis* PACIFIC OCEAN and HAWAII Killer Whale *Orcinus orca*
ATLANTIC OCEAN (see Chart 2)

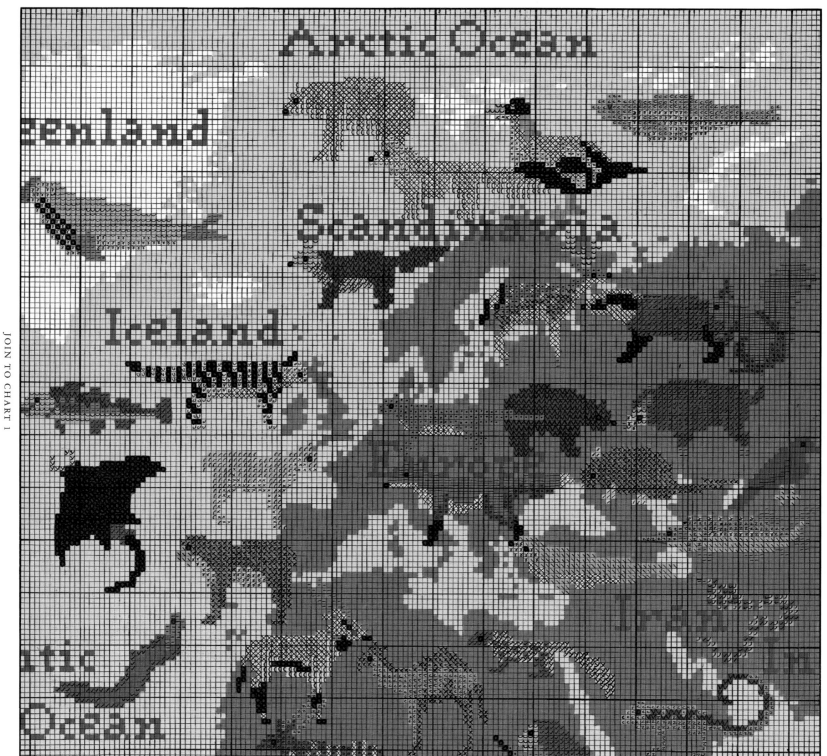

JOIN TO CHART 1

JOIN TO CHART 3

JOIN TO CHART 5

CHART 2 Contents: **ARCTIC OCEAN** Polar Bear *Thalarctos maritimus* Arctic Fox *Alopex lagopus* Bearded Seal *Erignathus barbatus*
GREENLAND Hooded Seal *Cystophora cristata* **SCANDINAVIA** Eider Duck *Somateria mollisima* Pine Marten *Martes martes*
EUROPE Wild Cat *Felis sylvestris* Weasel *Mustela nivalis* Fallow Deer *Dama dama* Badger *Meles meles* Red Squirrel *Sciurus vulgaris* Wild Boar *Sus scrofa*
Brown Bear *Ursus arctos* Spanish Lynx *Felis lynx* Barbary Ape *Macaca sylvanus* Red Fox *Vulpes vulpes* Dormouse *Muscardinus avellanarius*
Red Avadavat *Amandava amandava* Beluga *Huso huso* **INDIA** and **IRAN** Cobra *Naja naja* Monk Seal *Monachus monachus* **AFRICA** Chameleon *Chamaeleo chamaeleon*
Addax *Addax nasomaculatus* Dromedary *Camelus dromedarius* Spiny-tailed Agama *Uromastix acanthinurus* Gorilla *Gorilla gorilla* Bongo *Tragelaphus euryceros*
ATLANTIC OCEAN and **ICELAND** Conger Eel *Conger conger* Atlantic Manta *Manta birostris* Haddock *Melanogrammus aeglefinus*

CHART 3 Contents: **ARCTIC OCEAN** Bowhead Whale *Balaena mysticetus* Northern Bottlenose Whale *Hyperoodon ampullatus* Cod *Gadus morhua*
SIBERIA Siberian Lemming *Lemmus sibiricus* **ASIA** Sable *Martes zibellina* Reindeer *Rangifer tarandus* Snowy Owl *Nyctea scandiaca* Red Panda *Ailurus fulgens*
MONGOLIA Hamster *Cricetus cricetus* Wolf *Canis lupus* Arctic Ground Squirrel *Spermophilus parryi*
CHINA Giant Panda *Ailuropoda melanoleuca* Bactrian Camel *Camelus bactrianus* Onager *Equus hemionus*
Snow Leopard *Panthera uncia* Long-eared Jerboa *Euchoreutes naso* **INDIA** Tiger *Panthera tigris* Indian Elephant *Elephas maximus*
JAPAN Yellow-finned Tuna *Thunnus albacares* **PACIFIC OCEAN** Hammerhead Shark *Sphyrna zygaena*
Humpbacked Dolphin *Sousa chinensis* Blue Shark *Prionace glauca* Starry Flounder *Platichthys stellatus*
Whale Shark *Rhincodon typus* Sardine *Sardina pilchardus* Saury *Scomberesox saurus*

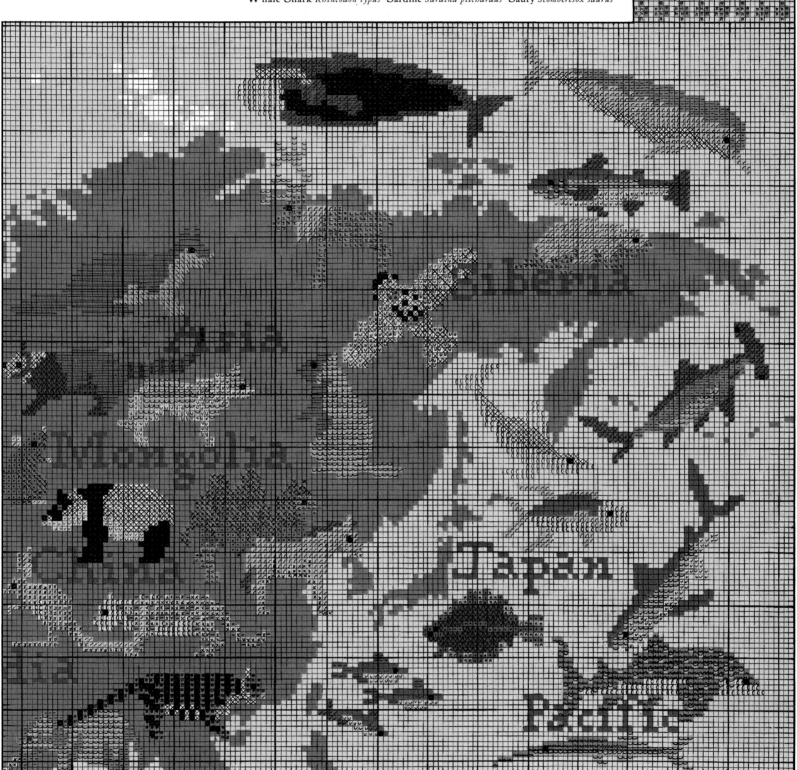

JOIN TO CHART 2

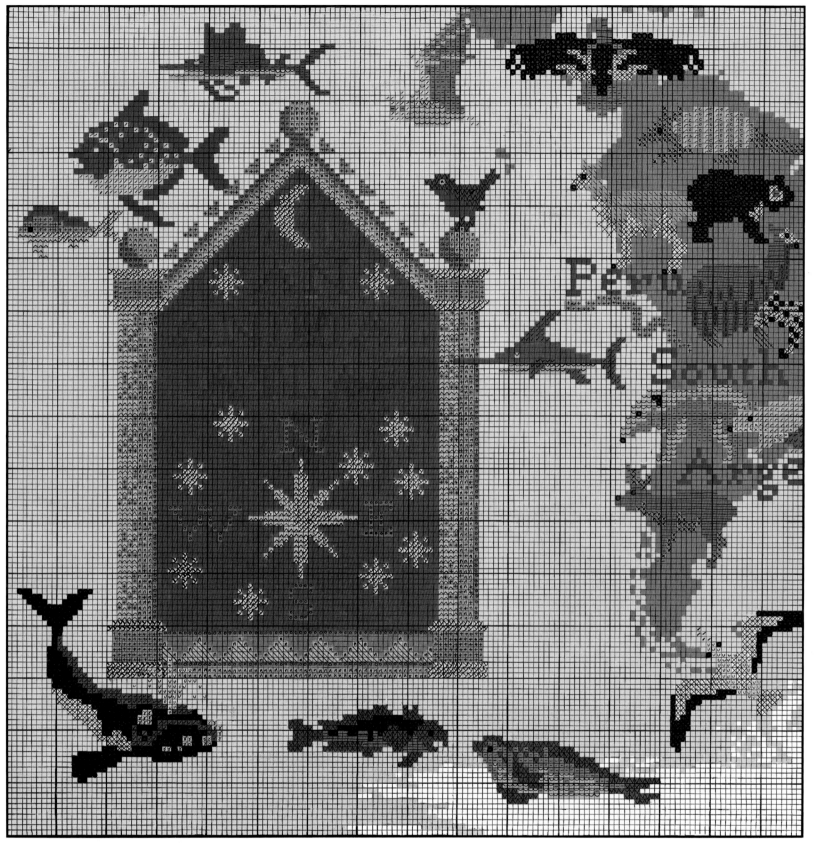

CHART 4 Contents: **SOUTH AMERICA and PERU** **V**ampire **B**at *Desmodus rotundus* **C**ondor *Vultur gryphus* **G**iant **A**rmadillo *Priodontes giganteus*
Vicuna *Vicugna vicugna* **S**pectacled **B**ear *Tremarctos ornatos* **A**lpaca *Lama pacos* **T**apir *Tapirus pinchaque* **C**hinchilla *Chinchilla laniger*
ARGENTINA **P**udu *Pudu mephistopheles* **ANTARCTICA** **A**lbatross *Diomedea exulans* **A**ntarctic **C**od *Notothenia coriiceps* **C**rabeater **S**eal *Lobodon carcinophagus*
AN ANIMAL ATLAS **R**obin *Erithacus rubecula* **PACIFIC OCEAN** **S**ailfish *Istiophorus platypterus* **O**pah *Lampris guttatus* **D**orado *Coryphaena hippurus*
Swordfish *Xiphias gladius* **H**umpback **W**hale *Megaptera novaeangliae*

CHART 5 Contents: SOUTH AMERICA and BRAZIL Grey Rhea *Rhea americana* Jaguar *Panthera onca* Red Howler Monkey *Alouatta seniculus*
Giant Anteater *Myrmecophaga tridactyla* ARGENTINA (see Chart 4) ATLANTIC OCEAN Atlantic Flying Fish *Cypselurus heterurus* Loggerhead Turtle *Caretta caretta*
Bluefish *Pomatomus saltatrix* Tripletail *Lobotes surinamensis* SOUTH ATLANTIC OCEAN Atlantic Torpedo or Electric Ray *Torpedo nobiliana*
Striped Dolphin *Stenella coeruleoalba* Minke Whale *Balaenoptera acutorostrata* ANTARCTICA Elephant Seal *Mirounga leonina* Chinstrap Penguin *Pygoscelis antarctica*
Emperor Penguin *Aptenodytes forsteri* Gentoo Penguin *Pygoscelis papua* AFRICA Gaboon Viper *Bitis gabonica* Wildebeest *Connochaetes taurinus*
Rhinoceros *Diceros bicornis* Hippopotamus *Hippopotamus amphibius* Lion *Panthera leo* Zebra *Equus burchelli* Cheetah *Acinonyx jubatus* Giraffe *Giraffa camelopardalis*
African Elephant *Loxodonta africana* Giant Golden Mole *Chrysospalax trevelyani* MADAGASCAR Parsons Chameleon *Chamaeleo parsonii* Ring-tailed Lemur *Lemur catta*
Ruffed Lemur *Varecia variegata* INDIAN OCEAN Coelacanth *Latimeria chalumnae*

CHART 6 Contents: **INDONESIA** Tapir *Tapirus indicus* Proboscis Monkey *Nasalis larvatus* **PACIFIC OCEAN** Pufferfish *Lagocephalus lagocephalus*
Blue-winged Octopus *Hapalochlaena maculosa* White Shark *Carcharodon carcharias* Batfish *Platax pinnatus* **INDIAN OCEAN** Ocean Sunfish *Mola mola*
AUSTRALIA Esturine Crocodile *Crocodilus porosus* Emu *Dromaius novaehollandiae* Red Kangaroo *Macropus rufus* Black Swan *Cygnus atratus*
Rainbow Lorikeet *Trichoglossus haematodus* Wombat *Lasiorhinus latifrons* Dingo *Canis dingo* Frilled Lizard *Chlamydosaurus kingii*
TASMANIA Tasmanian Devil *Sarcophilus harrisi* Platypus *Ornithorhynchus anatinus* Tiger Cat *Dasyurops maculatus* Red-bellied Pademelon *Thylogale billardierii*
Thylacine *Thylacinus cynocephalus* **NEW ZEALAND** Kiwi *Apteryx australis* Kakapo *Strigops habroptilus* New Zealand Sealion *Phocarctos hookeri*
Short-tailed Bat *Mystacina tuberculata* **SOUTHERN OCEAN** Blue Whale *Balenoptera musculus* **ANTARCTICA** Adelie Penguin *Pygoscelis adeliae*
Leopard Seal *Hydrurga leptonyx*

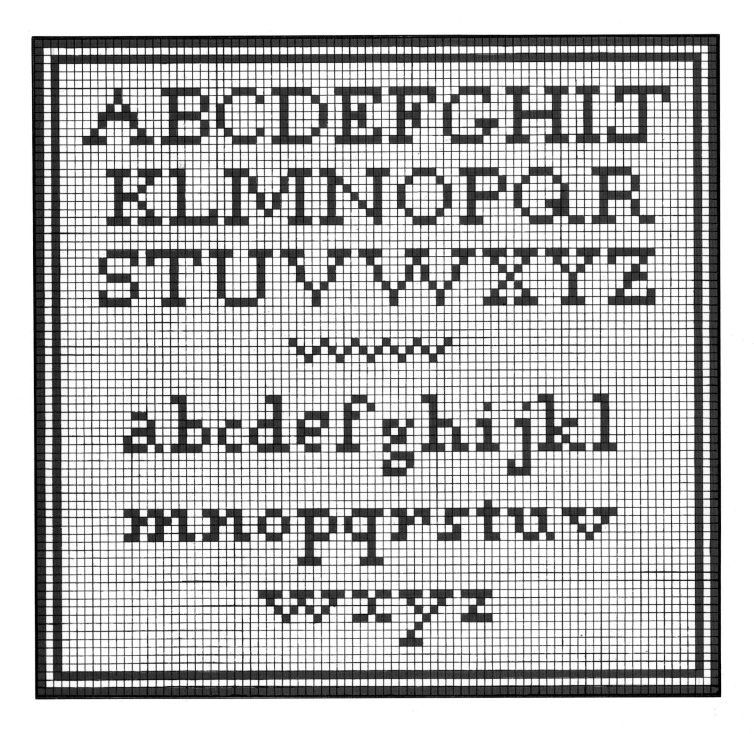

A chart showing the alphabet that has been
used on all the Animal Atlas charts. Names
of additional countries can be added where
desired using these letters.

LEFT: *The completed Animal Atlas carpet with border.*
This carpet has not been finished or edged.

CHAPTER TWO

Animals of the Air

Butterflies

Out of all the animals on this planet, butterflies are probably the most decorative and the easiest to represent through the medium of needlework. When at rest or laid out flat on a piece of paper they are already virtually two-dimensional and the bright colours and clearly defined patterns on their wings translate perfectly into the squared format of a needlework chart. The shape of even the plainest butterfly is attractive, with the symmetrical wings on either side of a roughly cylindrical body making it pleasing to the eye; even the two distinct antennae act as an interesting detail.

In the past, collecting butterflies, moths and beetles was a popular hobby. The insects were caught in butterfly nets, killed in a killing jar and then mounted with a pin through the thorax in a display case. The butterflies were either arranged in rows or assembled into elaborate patterns. Sometimes the cases were enclosed in specially made chests of drawers which can now occasionally be found tucked away in libraries or the forgotten corners of old houses.

Today, nobody would dream of killing butterflies merely as a genteel pastime or to add to a collection, or even just for the pleasure of arranging them into complex patterns in a specimen case. Old displays are often extremely pretty, however, and there is really no reason why they should not be used as decoration. In my years as an antique dealer I acquired several old cases made of mahogany with the finely dovetailed corners protected by brass mounts. They were filled with intricate arrangements of butterflies, moths and beetles and looked most attractive hung on the wall. This Butterfly needlework design was inspired by memories of such pieces as much as by the beauty of the insects themselves, their arrangement against a plain background is especially reminiscent of a classic antique butterfly display.

Collectors tended to group butterflies together into categories such as habitats, or country of origin or the variations of colour in a species. The butterflies selected for this design are all from Europe. Although it was tempting to include some of the magnificent and exotic butterflies which live in the tropics, I resisted because the resulting brilliantly coloured mix would have seemed contrary to the feel of the design. This rather restrained display seemed more authentic and suitable.

PREVIOUS PAGE: Real, but now deceased, butterflies that were bred in captivity flutter among needlework butterflies and a selection of leaves and flowers taken from the hedgerow. The stool top on the left has been worked in pink (A2) while the butterfly panel on the right has been worked in the slightly darker pink (A3).

OVERLEAF: Collage: butterflies and bees hover around a classic arrangement of garden flowers in a basket.

THE BUTTERFLIES

The butterflies listed below follow the order of those on the chart. Read the rows from left to right running down from top to bottom.

Swallowtail
Papilio machaon

Green Underside Blue
Glaucopsyche alexis

Black-veined White
Aporia crataegi

Purple Emperor
Apatura iris

Two-tailed Pasha
Charaxes jasius

Clouded Yellow
Colias crocea

Small White
Pieris rapae

Marbled White
Melanargia galathea

Brimstone
Gonepteryx rhamni

Wood White
Leptidea sinapis

Camberwell Beauty
Nymphalis antiopa

Green Hairstreak
Callophrys rubi

Peacock
Inachis io

Monarch
Danaus plexippus

Queen of Spain Fritillary
Argynnis lathonia

Alcon Blue
Maculinea alconides

Orange Tip
Anthocharis cardamines

Chalkhill Blue
Lysandra coridon

1 2 3 4 5 6 7 8 9 10 11 12 13 14 15 16 17 18 19 20 21 22 23 24 25 26 27

WOOL COLOURS AND QUANTITIES

The quantities listed below are the numbers of yards of Elizabeth Bradley wool needed to work a piece measuring 160 stitches by 160 stitches on 10 mesh interlock canvas using cross stitch.

Colours used:

27 including one background colour

The background colour of the piece shown on page 27 is pink (A3) and the background colour of the pieces used to cover the stool below is pale pink (A2).

Number on chart key	Elizabeth Bradley wool colours	Quantity (yards)
1	A3	184
2	B10	3
3	C1	8
4	C3	6
5	C5	9
6	C6	8
7	C7	21
8	C8	25
9	D2	13
10	D3	7
11	D4	13
12	E3	4
13	E8	6
14	E9	13
15	F3	34
16	F7	7
17	F9	25
18	F11	8
19	G2	10
20	G7	8
21	G10	84
22	H3	11
23	H10	9
24	J10	6
25	L9	9
26	L10	10
27	E2	6

Key number 1
is the background colour.

Suitable background colours

This design would work well with a number of background colours, particularly pastel shades. The pinks (A2 and A3) are both illustrated but cream (F3), pale greens (J2 or J3) and pale blue (L1) would all look attractive. Brighter but traditional colours such as grass green (J6) or saxe blue (L10) would make rich backgrounds suitable for a library or a study. Dark coloured or black backgrounds should be avoided because the dark brown (G10), which is used extensively throughout the design, would not show up against them.

Suggested projects

This is the last design that I painted for this book and it is one of my favourites. It is bright and fresh and would add colour and interest to all sorts of different rooms in a house. Horizontal strips of butterfly squares would look pretty covering a bedhead and individual butterflies could be worked as pincushions or on glasses cases or even worked in rows to make a border for a stool or rug.

Finished squares would make very pretty cushions or bolsters as well as stool and seat covers. A small stool like the one featured below can be useful either as a footrest or as an extra seat for children, cats or small dogs. This particular one is a copy of a Georgian stool. It is easy to upholster and makes a handsome and worthwhile project. Here the stool has been covered with the Butterflies design worked on a pale pink (A2) background. The top is covered with the completed square and the sides with a selection of the butterflies from the chart worked as a border.

If you would like to make a larger panel or rug from this design, extend it by working the squares, one next to the other, with no gap in between. Squares can be added both vertically and horizontally until the required size has been reached. The resulting carpet or panel, made up of adjoining Butterfly squares, should look both rich and unusual.

ABOVE: A small footstool covered with the Butterfly design worked with a pale pink (A2) background. The sides show a selection of butterflies extracted from the chart.

Parrot Chain

These four little parrots cannot be said to be any one definite species but rather resemble any number of small parrots or parakeets in their shapes, postures and brilliantly coloured plumage. Pet parrots often sit on rings suspended in their cages or from the ceiling rather than on wooden perches. The idea of extending a ring into a long chain was suggested by a small Victorian Berlin woolwork chart that is part of my collection, it can be made even longer by working more links and more parrots. The long strip of needlework shown to the left, worked on a black (G11) background, illustrates how this is done. The first and the fifth parrots are the same bird and so the repeat sequence from the bottom upwards goes: parrot one, two, three, four and five, then again parrots two, three, four and five and so on to make a strip of parrots as long as you want.

Parrots have been popular as pets ever since they were first discovered in the New World. They are easy to tame and are engaging and amusing birds. Added to their other charms is their ability to mimic the human voice. They will copy, not only simple words, but whole sentences and sequences of sounds. An uncle of a friend of mine had a parrot who was able to reproduce the noises made by him entering the house and settling into his armchair. First, the sound made by his key in the lock and then the door opening, the footsteps and last of all the groaning of the chair springs. Other parrots mimic doorbells, ringing telephones, swearing and favourite sayings and phrases, sometimes to the great embarrassment of their owner.

WOOL COLOURS AND QUANTITIES

The quantities listed below are the numbers of yards of Elizabeth Bradley wool needed to work a piece measuring 70 stitches by 276 stitches on 10 mesh interlock canvas using cross stitch.

Colours used:
16 plus one background colour

The background of the long Parrot Chain shown to the left is black (G11) and the background of the short Parrot Chain shown on page 34 is cream (F3).

Number on chart key	Elizabeth Bradley wool colours	Quantity (yards)
1	A6	14
2	B11	9
3	C5	4
4	C6	10
5	C9	12
6	C10	18
7	D7	10
8	H8	10
9	H10	9
10	I1	10
11	J10	14
12	J11	9
13	M2	6
14	M3	6
15	N7	3
16	N11	7

Background quantity for a piece measuring 70 stitches by 276 stitches: 218 yards.

LEFT: A chain of parrots worked on a black (G11) background.

Funnily enough, they do not appear to mimic either noises or the sounds made by other animals in the wild.

Pet parrots can become very possessive and jealous. They demand their owner's attention and will sometimes attack anyone and anything that they regard as competition; girlfriends, spouses or even your latest novel or the telephone can be in danger of a sharp peck if your parrot gets upset. They can also be quite destructive and do serious damage to furniture and room fittings if they get bored or feel neglected.

In spite of such drawbacks, parrots have great charm and some species are so much in demand that their survival is seriously threatened. The most beautiful and colourful birds are naturally the most coveted. Large birds like cockatoos, grey parrots and macaws are still captured from the wild and species that are particularly colourful – such as the golden shouldered parrot and the red fronted, hyacinth and blue headed macaws – are especially endangered.

Parrots in their natural environment

There are 315 species of parrots which range in size from 4 ins (10 cms) to 39 ins (99 cms), and they all bear a strong resemblance to each other both outwardly and in their physiology. They are divided into three families: there are 54 species of brush tongued lories,

18 species of cockatoos and all the rest are true parrots. Most parrots are brightly coloured and they all have short and sharply hooked beaks which are hinged at the top. These are so strongly muscled and powerful that they can be used like a third limb for climbing and feeding.

Parrots live in many tropical and subtropical regions but most species are found in Australia and the Amazon basin. They are gregarious birds living in large flocks and they can make an unbelievable din as they scream and screech and call to one another.

Parrots as pets

If parrots could be caught easily and transported without damaging a single one then their capture from their natural habitats would be less of a problem. This, however, is not what happens and instead a high proportion or even whole consignments of birds die while in transit. Great efforts have been made to restrict the import of parrots from the wild and the capture of protected species has been banned. To try to meet the demand from the pet trade some suitable species of parrots, such as lovebirds and cockatiels, are hatched and reared by hand. There are also several breeding programmes underway that are attempting to breed the rarest species and also introduce the captive bred birds back into the wild.

LEFT: A chain of parrots worked as shown on the chart on page 33. They have been worked on a cream (F3) background.

RIGHT: Collage: parrots and tropical birds perched among flowering branches.

Tawny Owl

It is the tawny owl (*Strix aluco*) that says "too-whit-to-whoo", the classic hoot that children learn in the nursery along with sheep saying "baaaa" and cows saying "moo". To be truthful, their call actually sounds more like "hoo...hooo. hoo. hooooooo....." or sometimes "kee-wick" in the autumn. The tawny owl is the commonest and most widespread of all British owls, and the most successful. Its natural habitat is woodland but it seems to live quite happily in large trees, whether on farms or in parks and gardens. It likes to make its nest in deep holes, finding hollow trees the perfect nesting site, but it will use crevices in rocks or even abandoned rabbit burrows. The eggs are large and white and are laid with an interval of a week between each so that the young vary considerably in size.

Owls are silent in flight, gliding noiselessly through the woods until they swoop, grab their prey in their powerful claws and carry it off to their favourite roost to devour in peace. They also hunt by sitting motionless on a branch and then dropping silently on top of unsuspecting wood mice, bank voles, frogs and small birds. Owls have favourite perches either to hunt from or to rest on during the day. These are easily identified because the ground beneath them becomes littered with their distinctive pellets, which are neat regurgitated parcels full of undigested prey.

The tawny owl's plumage is very soft and varies considerably in colour, ranging from a rich rusty brown to grey. The wings and back are mottled brown and grey while the breast is much paler and streaked with characteristic dark brown markings. The black eyes are set into a large round head, its legs and feet are feathered.

The Tawny Owl set in a fire screen

In our shop in Beaumaris on Anglesey, we are frequently asked if we have any designs which would be suitable to put in a fire screen. This life-size tawny owl should fit most fire screens. Its size can be adjusted by working more or less of the background until the required area has been covered.

LEFT: The Tawny Owl looks handsome in this Edwardian fire screen. It has been worked on a pale blue (L1) background.

RIGHT: Collage: tawny owls in a bluebell wood.

WOOL COLOURS AND QUANTITIES

The quantities listed below are the numbers of yards of Elizabeth Bradley wool needed to work a piece measuring 172 stitches by 210 stitches on 10 mesh interlock canvas using cross stitch.

Colours used:

25 including one background colour

Number on chart key	Elizabeth Bradley wool colours	Quantity (yards)
1	C3	5
2	C5	9
3	C6	8
4	E5	13
5	E8	23
6	E11	25
7	F3	11
8	F5	13
9	F6	23
10	F7	40
11	F8	4
12	F10	14
13	G8	23
14	G10	3
15	H2	9
16	H4	9
17	I2	5
18	I5	10
19	I9	9
20	I11	10
21	J6	25
22	J8	21
23	J10	11
24	K7	12
25	L1	420

Key number 25
is the background colour.

ABOVE: The Tawny Owl worked on a pale blue (L1) background.

Fire screens, far from being obsolete in the 1990s, are much in demand. Most older houses and quite a few new ones have open fires, and fireplaces that have been blocked for the last fifty years are being unblocked all over the country. All sorts of smart mantelpieces, surrounds, grates and baskets are being manufactured and often the only thing missing from the well-furnished fireplace is the fire screen.

An attractive fire screen is actually quite difficult to acquire. A selection of modern and reproduction pieces are manufactured and can be bought in many needlework shops. On the whole, I find older examples more appealing and would always have a good rummage around salerooms and in antique shops before buying a modern example.

| 1 | 2 | 3 | 4 | 5 | 6 | 7 | 8 | 9 | 10 | 11 | 12 | 13 | 14 | 15 | 16 | 17 | 18 | 19 | 20 | 21 | 22 | 23 | 24 | 25 |

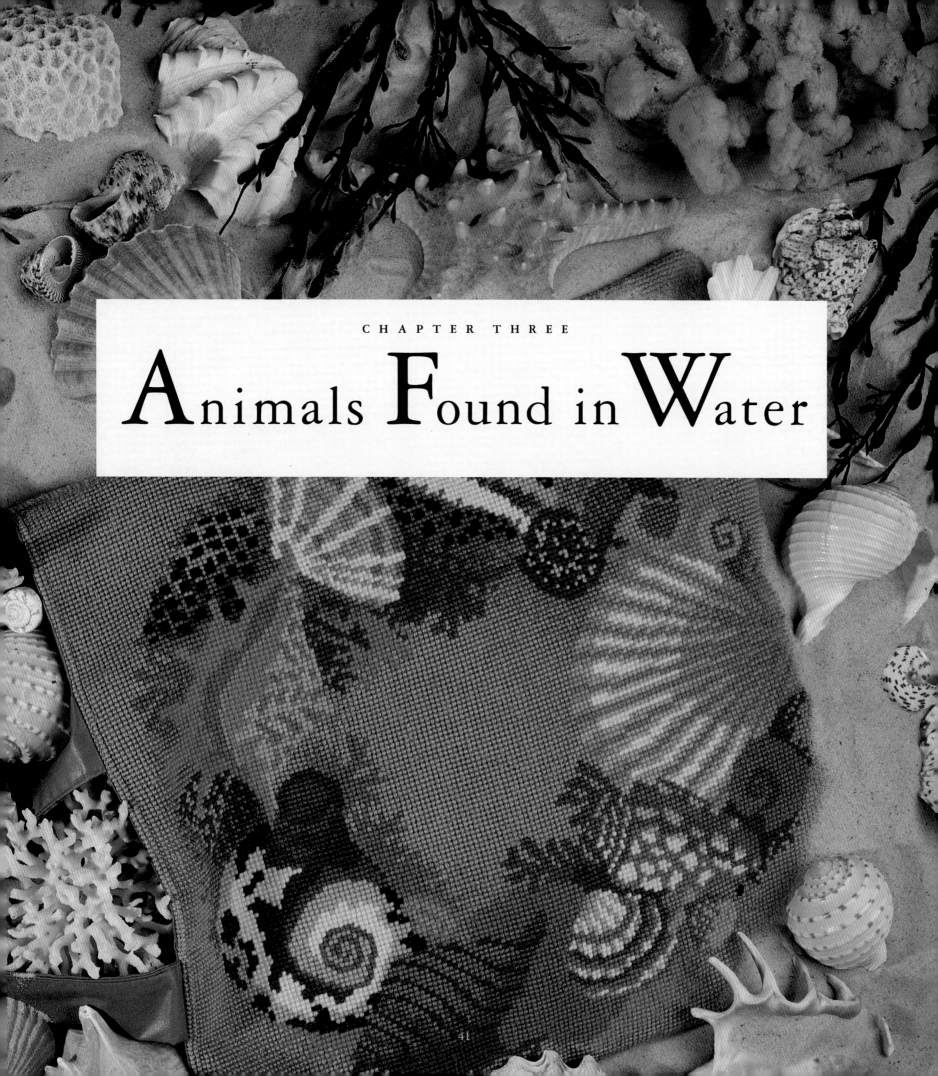

CHAPTER THREE

Animals Found in Water

Shell Wreath

Because shells are pretty and varied in their shapes and colours they make ideal ornaments around the house. They are so perfect for decorating a plain mirror frame, for putting on a coffee table, or arranging in a basket in the bathroom, that it is sometimes hard to remember that they were once animals living at the bottom of the sea. The shell was made by the creature that lived inside it; it is the external skeleton of a soft-bodied organism called a mollusc.

Most molluscs belong to two main classes, gastropods (which have one-piece coiled shells) and bivalves (which have a two-piece shell held together with a hinge). The creation of a shell begins with a tiny mollusc egg which hatches into a larva that may swim around among the plankton on the surface of the sea for several months before it settles on the sea floor. As it grows bigger, the mollusc develops tentacles, eyes, a proboscis, and also a muscular fleshy foot with which it moves. It resembles a snail which is, of course, a species of mollusc adapted to living on land.

As it feeds and grows, the mollusc secretes a hard covering of calcium carbonate and protein around itself and this is the shell. Each species produces a characteristic shape and colour of shell. A tiny cockle shell is essentially identical to the shell of a juicy mature cockle, but just a lot smaller.

Like most groups of animals, marine molluscs have adapted to a wide variety of habitats. Some live on rocks covered only at high tide, others on sandy beaches, or in deep oozy mud. Some are found only on coral reefs while others attach themselves to piers or quays or even ships. The conditions found in the tropics are particularly ideal for molluscs and this is where the biggest and most spectacular shells come from.

Because of their beauty, shells are highly collectible. They are gathered for their scientific interest or to add to already existing collections, sadly they are also acquired in vast quantities just because they are so lovely to look at. They are naturally occurring, decorative objects so perfect for display, that one forgets that the animals inside have to be killed for us to have them. Sadly the supply of shells is not inexhaustible and some species are already becoming very rare.

One good thing about shells is that they are extremely durable and do not become less beautiful with age. We could stop harvesting tropical shells tomorrow and still have millions to recycle and enjoy in our houses for many years to come. Victorian shell pictures and boxes are as charming and fresh as when they were first made.

If large quantities of fresh shells are needed, then there are lots of empty ones lying around to be picked up and used. Their mollusc owners have died, or in some cases been eaten, and the shells are there ready to be enjoyed. Well-known collecting venues, like Shell Beach on Herm in the Channel Islands, have been denuded of all but the smaller shells, but there are plenty here in North Wales if you look for them on the less well-walked beaches.

WOOL COLOURS AND QUANTITIES

The quantities listed below are the numbers of yards of Elizabeth Bradley wool needed to work a piece measuring 160 stitches by 160 stitches on 10 mesh interlock canvas using cross stitch.

Colours used:
26 plus one background colour

The background colour of the piece shown on page 44 is cream (F3) and the background colour of the piece used to make the bag on page 41 is pale blue (L1).

Number on chart key	Elizabeth Bradley wool colours	Quantity (yards)
1	A3	9
2	A9	7
3	B2	17
4	B3	16
5	B4	17
6	B7	18
7	C1	15
8	C3	9
9	C6	12
10	C7	9
11	C9	18
12	C10	3
13	E4	10
14	E8	4
15	E10	9
16	F3	29
17	F7	17
18	G1	9
19	G5	6
20	G7	13
21	H2	13
22	H3	9
23	I1	18
24	I5	18
25	N1	11
26	N3	10

Background quantity for a piece measuring 160 stitches by 160 stitches: 200 yards.

PREVIOUS PAGE: *Shell Wreaths surrounded by shells, seaweed and sand. The wreath on the left has been worked on a cream (F3) background while the Shell Wreath workbag on the right has a pale blue (L1) background.*

1 2 3 4 5 6 7 8 9 10 11 12 13 14 15 16 17 18 19 20 21 22 23 24 25 26

ABOVE: A Shell Wreath worked on a cream (F3) background.
The frame has been whitened with a thin coat of white acrylic paint before being polished.

THE SHELLS

Working around the wreath in a clockwise direction from the scallop shell at the bottom, the shells in the wreath are:

Queen Scallop
Aequipecten opercularis

Boat Ear Moon
Sinum cymba

Noble Cone
Conus nobilis

Smooth Scallop
Chlamys glabra

Giant Cockle
Plagiocardium pseudolima

Common European Oyster
Ostrea edulis

Banded Tulip
Fasciolaria tulipa

Thin Tellin
Tellina tenuis

South African Turban
Turbo sarmaticus

Common Purple Sea Snail
Janthina janthina

Mottled Top
Trochus maculatus

Common Spider Conch
Lambis lambis

The Junonia
Scaphella junonia

Striped Tellin
Tellina virgata

Tiger Cowrie
Cypraea tigris

Tower Shell
Turritella communis

Needle Shell
Bittium reticulatum

Common Button Top
Umbonium vestiarium

Opal Jewel Top
Cantharidus opalus

Flat Periwinkle
Littorina littoralis

This design shows a wreath of shells. They are not from any particular area of the world but were chosen for their shapes and colours, and are set in a ring of corals and brightly coloured algae. The design was intended to be soft and pretty and yet highly decorative; a pink and blue pastel piece with touches of brighter colour. Aquamarine is a favourite background colour of mine; I particularly like it combined with pinks and rusts, soft oranges and beige and cream. One of the two finished pieces shown has been worked on such a pale blue (L1) background and the other on cream (F3) because it is such a useful and universal furnishing colour. Black (G11) is another such neutral colour and I imagine this wreath might look rather smart worked with a black background.

RIGHT: Collage: an elegant urn filled with shells and seaweed.

Sperm Whale Bath Mat

LEFT: This spouting Sperm Whale Bath Mat has been edged with black fabric cut on the cross and used like bias binding. It makes a firm and effective edging.

This whale design has been painted in a much more primitive style than is usual for me. I have always liked naive art and find the simple pictures of whaling scenes that were painted in America in the last century very appealing, in spite of the rather horrific nature of the subject matter. Another factor affecting the design's style was the nature of the beast itself; a detailed and delicately shaded Victorian representation would have been quite wrong for a whale, it is far too big and bold an animal to be treated fussily.

The sperm whale (*Physeter catodon*) is the species of whale most often seen in old prints and paintings. Its distinctive shape seems to me to be the classic and archetypal whale outline and so when trying to decide which whale to put on the bath mat, it came out clear favourite. The reason that the sperm whale was painted so often in the past is because, out of all the whales, it was the species most sought after by whaling fleets throughout the last century. Its huge square head is filled with a waxy substance called spermaceti which was highly prized. When heated, it yields a very pure oil which was used to make cosmetics as well as being a lubricant and lamp oil.

The sperm whale is a massive animal with large teeth in its lower jaw, and a mature male can grow as long as 59ft (18m) and live for 65-70 years. Whales are very well adapted to living underwater; their shape is stream-lined and they have a thick layer of blubber under the skin to keep their temperature constant in cold seas. Like all mammals, whales breathe air with lungs rather than acquiring their oxygen from the water through gills, like fish. Every now and again whales come to the surface and blow out the old, stale air from their lungs through a blow hole on the top of the head. The young are born underwater and the baby whale must take its first breath fairly quickly to survive. Sometimes other females will support the mother in the water and help the baby to the surface. The mother will suckle the young whale constantly for several months and then intermittently for up to 13 years.

Whales use sound both to communicate with each other and to locate underwater obstacles: invaluable when they are navigating in deep and dark ocean waters. If a whale 'shouts' loudly, as they sometimes do, it can be heard by another whale up to 50 miles (80km) away. Sperm whales also produce series of high frequency clicks which seem to be used for echolocation not only in order to map the contours of their surroundings but also to locate and even to stun shoals of fish and squid. It is thought that the spermaceti in a whale's skull cavity may cause the skull to act as a reverberation chamber, increasing the intensity of the sound pulses so that they are more effective in immobilizing prey.

The major item in a sperm whale diet is squid, with some octopus and fish. They will dive or 'sound' to great depths to feed, staying underwater for up to two hours. Dives of up to 9,750ft (3,000m) have been recorded and specimens of deep water squid as long as 39.4ft (12m) have been found in sperm whale stomachs. An adult male eats as much as 550 tonnes (550,000kg) of squid each year.

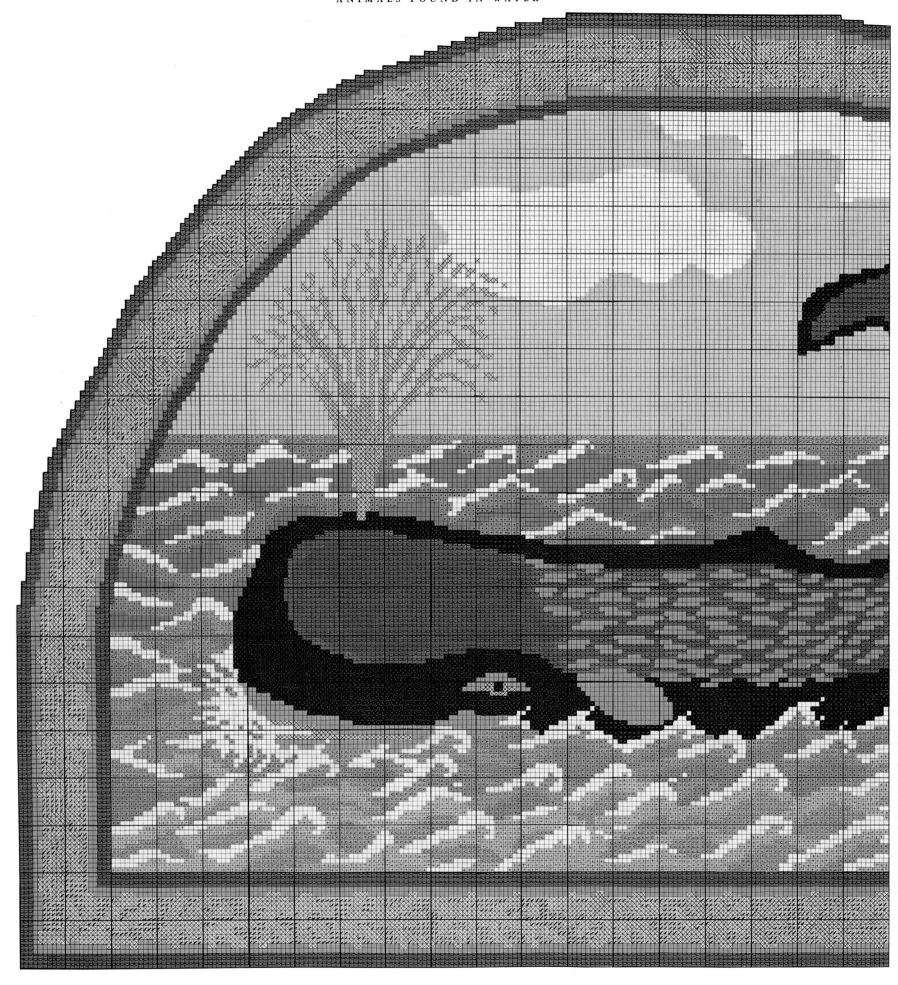

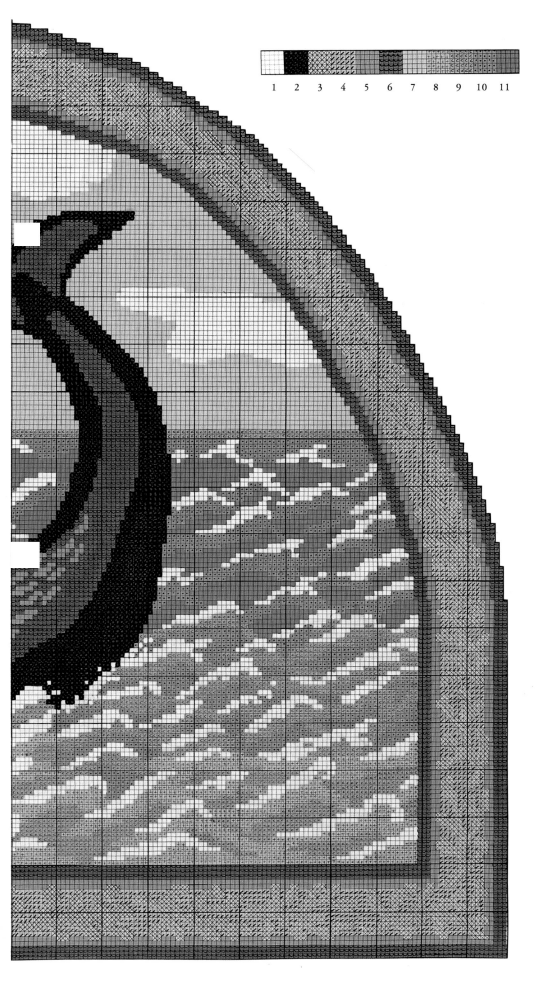

WOOL COLOURS AND QUANTITIES

The quantities listed below are the numbers of yards of Elizabeth Bradley wool needed to work a piece measuring 299 stitches by 200 stitches maximum on 10 mesh interlock canvas using cross stitch.

Colours used: 11 colours

Number on chart key	Elizabeth Bradley wool colours	Quantity (yards)
1	F1	132
2	G10	80
3	H6	193
4	H7	76
5	H9	84
6	H11	88
7	L1	132
8	L2	50
9	L3	84
10	L4	77
11	L5	50

The sperm whale in this design is blowing, or breathing out, in an explosive, vertical cloud of spray. He (or she) is swimming along in a choppy sea, with a brisk wind under a blue sky scattered with a few, fat cumulus clouds. The border surrounding the half-moon shaped picture is based on the knobbly branches of coral, grey and bleached as it is sometimes found washed up on the beach.

When stitched, this piece would make a most unusual bath mat though one might rather resent it getting wet after all that work; alternatively, it would look handsome (and keep dry) hung on a wall. It measures 29.9 ins (76 cms) across the bottom and so will fit across a piece of canvas 39 ins (1 m) wide. It is best started at the bottom and worked upwards until complete. To finish, trim the canvas to about 2 ins (5 cms) all the way around and then turn it under and stitch in place. Binding the edge with navy blue or black cotton material cut on the cross looks smart, rather like a stout, nautical bias binding.

Mackerel Glasses Case

Mackerel (*Scomber scombrus*), tuna, wahoos and bonito are all members of the same family, the Scombridae; they are all good to eat and many of them are superb game fish. They have probably the most perfectly streamlined body of all fish and are one of the fastest, cruising in large schools at 30 miles an hour. They are also predators and will attack other fish that they meet along their way.

In Britain, the mackerel seen in fish shops and known from fishing expeditions in late summer around the coast, are Atlantic mackerel. They eat mainly small crustaceans, shrimps, whitebait and pilchards rather than attacking larger fish. Although they are an oily fish, their flesh is firm and delicious. They are smoked in vast quantities and, in this form, are for sale in almost every supermarket. They are a successful fish and have a widespread distribution, each female producing about half a million eggs in her lifetime. Mackerel are handsome, with blue-green and black stripes above the lateral line and silver below. Their fins are spiny and soft rayed, the tail is much tapered and the scales are tiny and hardly noticeable.

BELOW: Pairs of mackerel have been made into glasses cases. They are worked on two different background colours: pink (A3) and green (J10).

OPPOSITE: Collage: shoals of mixed deep sea fish swim across the page.

Some uses for woolwork mackerel

Glasses or spectacles cases made from woolwork fulfil their purpose admirably. They protect the glasses and are pleasant to use. They also wear well, surviving life in a handbag for many years and they make excellent Christmas and birthday presents. Most glasses case designs are narrower than the one shown here but I like a glasses case to be lined and feel that it needs to be big enough to hold a pair of owl-like sunglasses if necessary. If you wear narrow, elegant glasses then stitch one fish only on each side of the case and work more background around it until the required size is reached.

It is always interesting to look at a design and ponder on other ways in which it could be useful. Looking at this one it seemed to me that it had potential as a repeating border. For instance, one of the mackerel could be repeated in a long line to produce a strip about 2 ins (5 cms) wide which might be useful to make belts or camera straps or even wide fishy braces. Alternatively, the design could be repeated downwards and a border 6.6 ins (7 cms) wide produced with alternate fish facing different directions. A mackerel bellpull made from such a strip might appeal to a fanatical fisherman for his study. Fishing is a particularly popular hobby and this means there are a lot of fishermen out there needing presents.

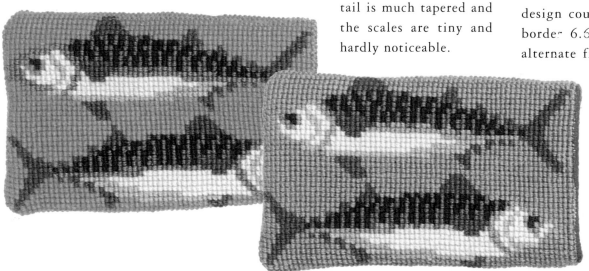

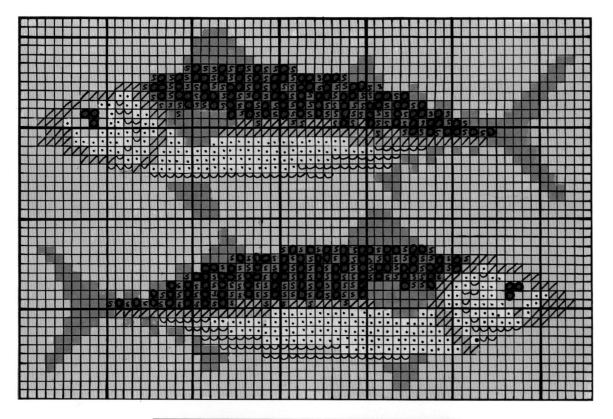

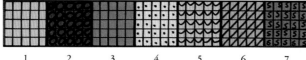

1   2   3   4   5   6   7

WOOL COLOURS AND QUANTITIES

The quantities listed below are the numbers of yards of Elizabeth Bradley wool needed to work a piece measuring 66 stitches by 42 stitches on 10 mesh interlock canvas using cross stitch.

To make a glasses case, two pieces of this size are needed.

Colours used:

7 including one background colour

The background colours of the two glasses cases shown on page 50 are green (J10) and pink (A3).

Number on chart key	Elizabeth Bradley wool colours	Quantity (yards)
1	D3	33
2	G10	4
3	H10	6
4	H6	7
5	H7	3
6	H9	4
7	K10	4

Key number 1
is the background colour.

The strip of horizontal mackerel shown opposite is worked with a blue (M6) background. The narrow mackerel line is worked with a coral (C9) background.

Making a lined glasses case

Place the two finished mackerel pieces with the right sides facing and machine stitch them together one stitch in from the edge of the needlework. Stitch all around three sides leaving one narrow edge open. Trim the canvas so that ½ in (12 mm) remains. Machine stitch two pieces of lining fabric together (the same size as the needlework pieces) in the same way but this time leaving both short edges open.

Turn the stitched needlework pieces through so that the right sides are facing outwards. Slip the stitched lining pieces over the needlework like a glove. Make sure that the right sides of the lining and the needle-work are facing and that one narrow edge of the lining is placed along the unstitched narrow edge of the needlework. Machine stitch the lining to the finished mackerel pieces around the narrow edges, one stitch in from the edge of the needlework.

Turn the lining through so that the right sides are on the outside. Hand stitch the remaining open end of the lining then tuck it inside the needlework pieces.

To stop the lining easing out of the top of the glasses case, machine stitch all the way around the open edge through both the needlework and the lining, one stitch in from the edge.

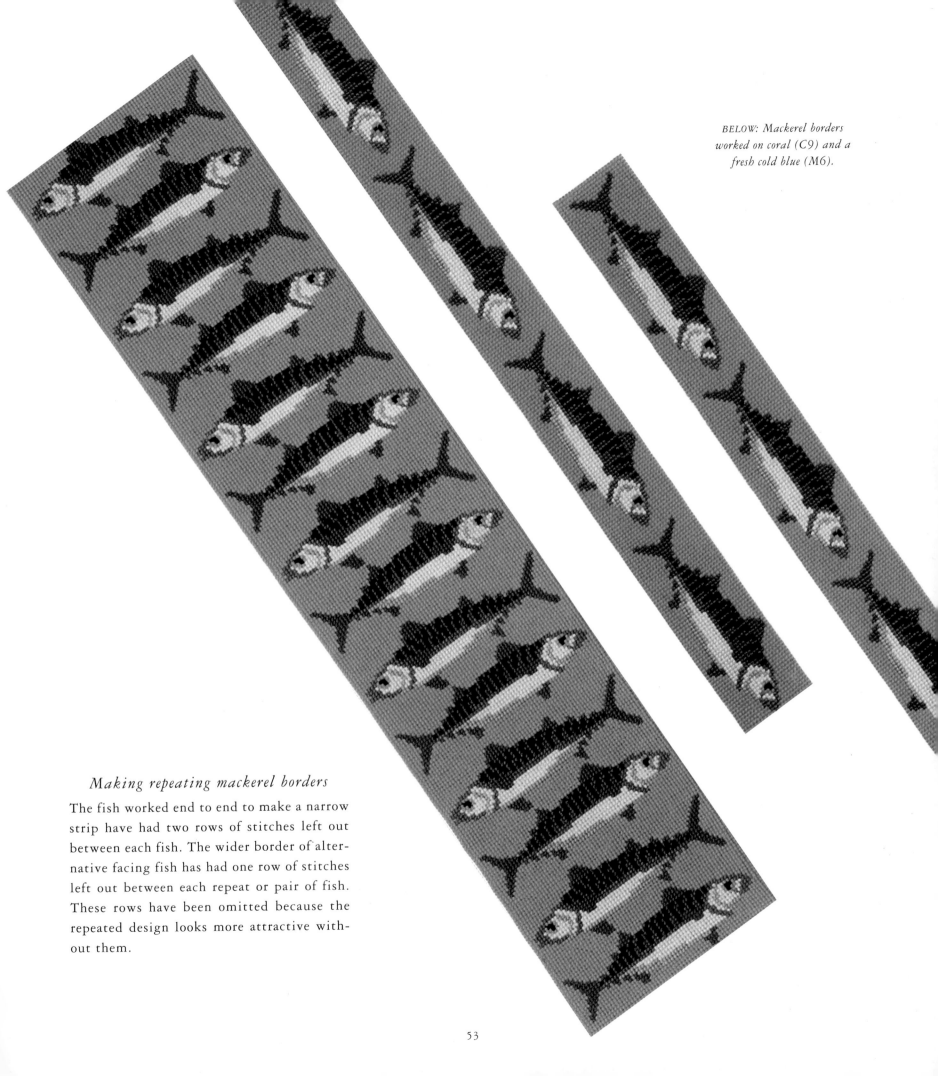

BELOW: *Mackerel borders worked on coral (C9) and a fresh cold blue (M6).*

Making repeating mackerel borders

The fish worked end to end to make a narrow strip have had two rows of stitches left out between each fish. The wider border of alternative facing fish has had one row of stitches left out between each repeat or pair of fish. These rows have been omitted because the repeated design looks more attractive without them.

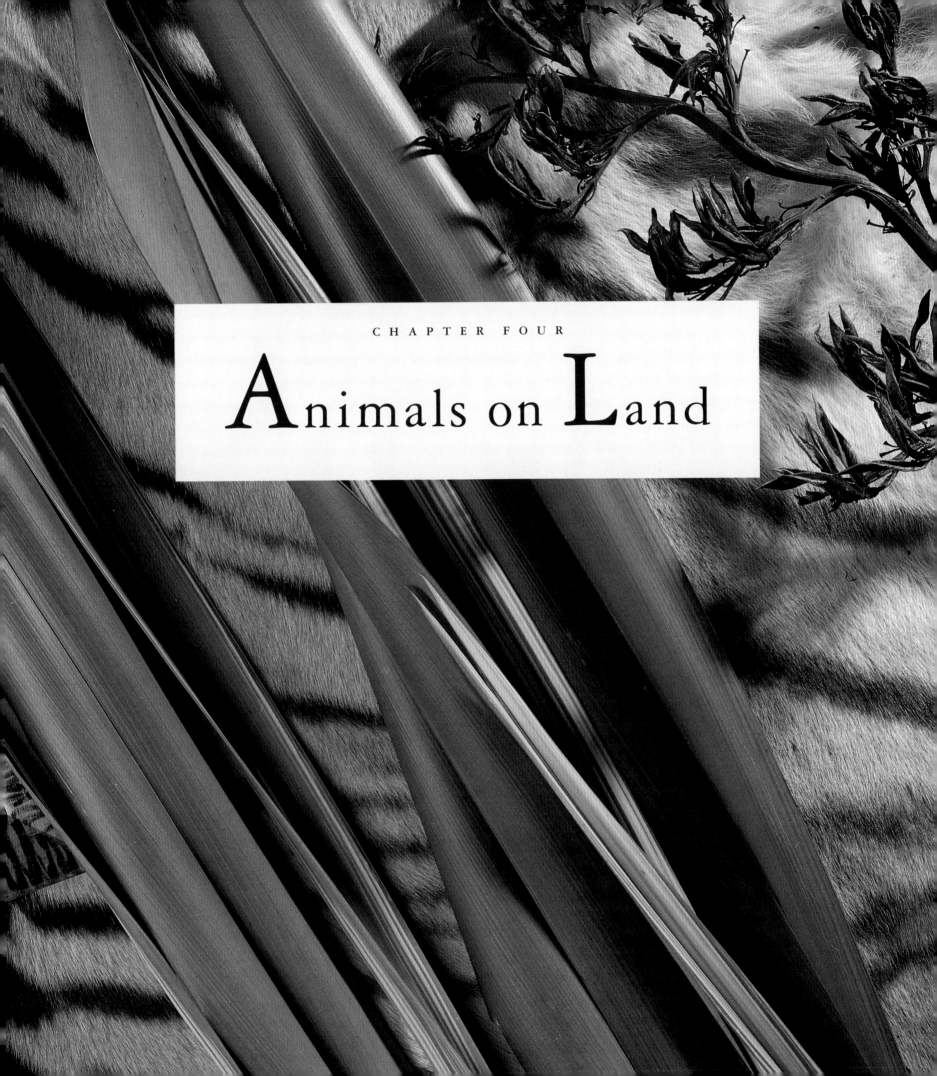

CHAPTER FOUR

Animals on Land

Fox Family Rug

The red fox (*Vulpes vulpes*), seems to be regarded either as a hero or a rogue, the viewpoint depending on the lifestyle of the individual. To a country man working with domestic animals and the land, he is a villain but also a bit of a lad – he is Tod, out to steal his chickens and geese if he can, and maybe kill a new born lamb or destroy a run of pheasant chicks. To a writer of fables and stories, he is clever and cunning – he is Reynard. To a nature lover he is beautiful and fascinating to observe, and to a fox hunter he is prey and an exciting day out. Whatever he is, the red fox is certainly a delight to look at though a little musky and pungent to smell at close quarters.

A fox is the largest British predator with an average fox being about 42 ins (107 cms) long from the end of its nose to the point of its white-tipped tail. Its fur is reddish brown or pale reddish in colour but with many different shades of brown and grey hair also present in the long, lustrous coat. The lower legs and the back of the ears are black. Foxes live in earths or dens which are often abandoned rabbit burrows or partly deserted badger setts; badger and fox cubs are sometimes seen playing together.

The fox is a very versatile and intelligent mammal with excellent senses and powers of endurance. Its sight is poor compared to a bird of prey but its hearing and senses of smell and touch are superb. The fox has a long, pointed and very sensitive snout and a

PREVIOUS PAGE: A stitched and framed Tiger has been photographed against the spiky leaves of Phormium tenax *laid across a magnificent antique, Siberian tiger skin belonging to the 74th Tiger Squadron of the RAF.*

brain with well developed olfactory lobes which allow it to see the world as a series of complex scent pictures: a perception that is difficult for us to imagine because our smelling ability is comparatively rudimentary. Foxes routinely mark their territory with scent-marks so strong that even we can smell them. A well developed sense of touch is very useful in the dark. Foxes have long sensitive whiskers (or vibrissae) sprouting from around their muzzles, eyes and chins as well as along both forelegs. These whiskers plus their sensitive ears and noses help a fox to be an almost perfect nocturnal hunter.

Foxes are successful animals and have a very widespread distribution. They can be found in Canada, the USA, Europe, Asia to Japan, Indo China and Australia. Their natural habitat is woodland, open country and similar terrain in urban areas; as a species they adapt well to different conditions. They are not fussy eaters and enjoy a wide variety of food. Their natural diet includes all sorts of rodents, rabbits, hares, moles and squirrels as well as birds and their eggs. They eat a lot of beetles in the summer and fruit and berries in the autumn. Foxes tend to be unpopular with farmers because although they eat rabbits which are a pest, they will also raid farmyards and chicken houses, and sometimes even attack young lambs. Maybe the secret of their success is that they are such great opportunists, eating almost anything that comes their way.

Town dwelling foxes are becoming increasingly common, breeding in gardens and parks. On the whole they are regarded benignly and with interest and are welcome in towns. They are useful in that they eat pests like rats, mice and voles and the problem of them also catching the odd cat and scattering the contents of an occasional dustbin is outweighed at the moment by the novelty of their presence.

The vixen's mating call is a high pitched, long drawn out, rather blood curdling scream which must sound extremely eerie ringing out over a suburban garden. Dog foxes bark and cubs can be quite noisy, yelping and chattering as they play. Foxes live alone except during the breeding season when they seem to develop strong family ties; the dog fox, mother fox and sometimes two or three non-breeding vixens live together for the summer until the cubs leave. Only the dominant vixen comes into season, mates and gives birth. Gestation is 51-63 days and an average of four cubs are born in each litter. The cubs are born blind and deaf and covered with short black fur. Once the cubs are born, the dog fox and supporting vixens will forage and bring food back to the family. By eight weeks they have become adventurous and by three months have begun to be independent.

BELOW: A corner of the border of the Fox Family Rug. This Victorian border is both adaptable and useful. It looks attractive around almost any type of central design. To reduce or expand its size, merely shorten or lengthen the plain rows of stitches that run between the ornate corners.

Fox Family Rug

This Fox Family Rug measures 29.8ins (75.5cms) by 20.8ins (53cms). It shows a vixen alert and ready for trouble with two cubs of about three months old. They are set in a rather park-like setting surrounded by rocky outcrops. It is late summer with the trees just beginning to change to their autumn colours.

This small carpet will fit easily across a piece of canvas that is 39ins (1m) wide. If stitching is started at the bottom right-hand corner of the piece, work the rows of stitches across the canvas from selvedge to selvedge.

If a slightly larger carpet is required, just work more rows of maroon (A9) edging on each of the four sides. I have shown a border of the minimum possible width on the chart so as to keep the scale of the chart as large as possible on the page but an extra inch, or even two added to each side of the rug would actually look very nice.

PREVIOUS PAGE: Collage: suburban foxes in a flowerbed.

WOOL COLOURS AND QUANTITIES

The quantities listed below are the numbers of yards of Elizabeth Bradley wool needed to work a piece measuring 298 stitches by 208 stitches on 10 mesh interlock canvas using cross stitch.

Colours used: 30 colours

Number on chart key	Elizabeth Bradley wool colours	Quantity (yards)
1	A7	200
2	C5	17
3	C6	10
4	E1	23
5	E3	23
6	E5	100
7	E8	138
8	E9	84
9	E11	18
10	G7	27
11	F3	23
12	G9	28
13	G10	24
14	H2	50
15	H3	54
16	I1	36
17	I2	63
18	I4	58
19	I9	57
20	I11	58
21	J3	40
22	J4	50
23	J5	33
24	J6	25
25	J10	23
26	J11	18
27	L1	121
28	N9	9
29	N10	18
30	N11	14

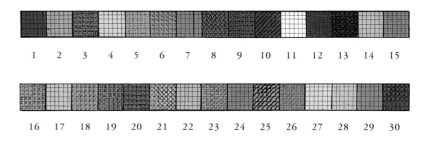

Carpet Python Draft Stopper

If you are fed up with chilly drafts whistling around your feet as you sit in an otherwise cosy room then this is the design for you. My studio in Beaumaris on Anglesey is a tiny, two room cottage. It is kept pleasantly warm but there is a cold draft that sweeps through it at floor level, coming in at the front door and swirling out through the back door opposite. I am depending on a pair of carpet pythons to keep my feet unfrozen this coming winter.

I was delighted to find that a snake with such a suitable name as a carpet python (*Morelia argus*), not only existed but would also make a splendid needlework design. Carpet pythons have the bold and distinct markings that I was looking for and are comparatively short and fat. A long thin snake like a cobra or an anaconda would look most odd shortened to a door width of approximately 3 ft (1 m). The carpet python is a common and widely distributed snake in Australia and New Guinea. It grows up to a length of 11 ft (3.4 m) and is usually found inland living in the forest or among scrub and bush. The dark patterning on its body mimics the leaves and debris in which the snake spends much of its time.

The carpet python is most active at night, resting during the day in holes or hollow tree stumps, but it can sometimes be seen basking in the sunshine. It eats small mammals and birds, killing them with its sharp teeth.

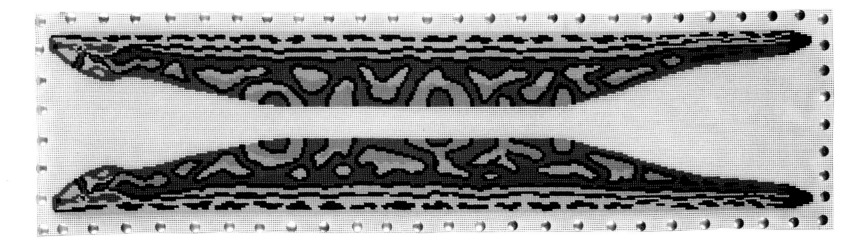

Finishing the Carpet Python

The carpet python is designed to be stitched in two parts like the finished pieces shown above. Work the charts with no overlap between them. Trim the seam allowance to ½ in (12mm), then sew together the two finished halves of the snake on a line which is one stitch in from the edge of each piece. They cannot be successfully machine stitched together as the snake is too narrow to be turned through neatly. Instead, join them together by hand with wrong sides facing using small stitches and strong thread. The best stitch for this is an upholstery stitch which is worked by making a stitch on the edge of each piece alternately. When the resulting zigzag of thread is pulled tightly (which should be done every few stitches), the two sides of the snake will be neatly drawn together.

Leave a gap along the centre of the stomach to insert the filling – acrylic wadding or any other type of soft toy filler works well. Pack the filling tightly into the body, making sure that it is pushed right up into the head and tail. Last of all, sew up the gap. The carpet python should be long enough for most doors; if it is too long, the tail can be made shorter by rounding it off earlier. Alternatively, it can be just bent up at a right angle in the doorway.

ABOVE: Two sections of stitched Carpet Python stretched out on a board before being joined as described on this page.

BELOW: A joined and stuffed Carpet Python ready to be put to good use when it is laid along the bottom of a door.

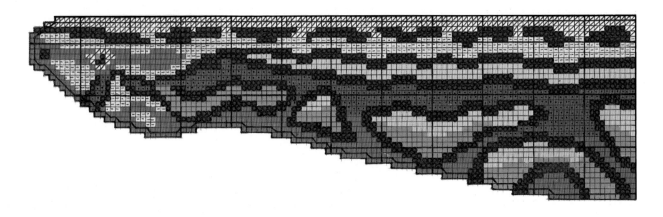

CHART 1

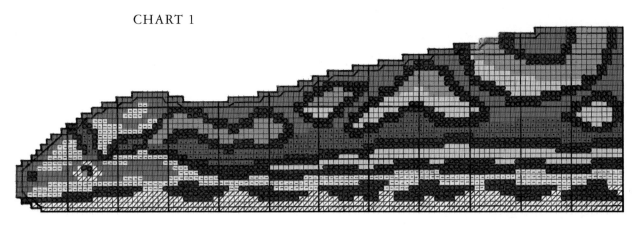

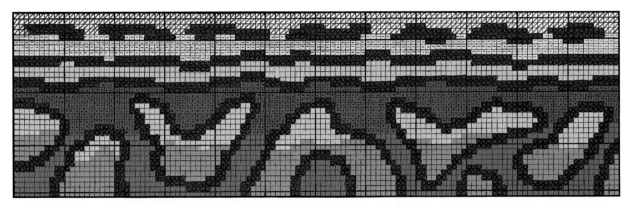

CHART 2

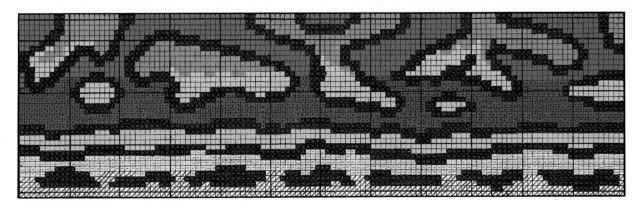

WOOL COLOURS AND QUANTITIES

The quantities listed below are the numbers of yards of Elizabeth Bradley wool need to work the two sides of the Carpet Python. Each side measures a maximum of 360 stitches by 35 stitches and is worked on 10 mesh interlock canvas using cross stitch.

Colours used: 7 colours

Number on chart key	Elizabeth Bradley wool colours	Quantity (yards)
1	C1	37
2	C2	38
3	C3	50
4	C5	39
5	C11	50
6	E9	46
7	G10	150

1   2   3   4   5   6   7

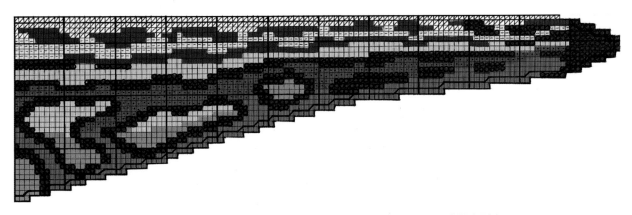

CHART 3

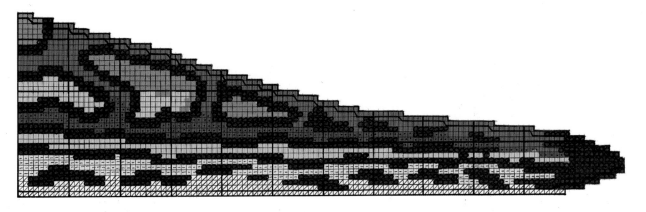

Tiger

When discussing tigers (*Panthera tigris*) perhaps it is as well to dispense with the negative facts before extolling the wonders of what is an animal of almost legendary beauty. First of all, tigers do kill and eat people, even if only very occasionally. Man does not seem to be a tiger's first choice of prey but nevertheless, once a tiger starts eating humans it tends to continue to do so and eventually man-eaters have to be hunted down and killed. Second, there are not many tigers left. Man has managed to kill most of them either for sport or because their interests conflict. In spite of our now earnest desire that the remnants of the species should survive and thrive there is considerable doubt whether this will be possible in today's overcrowded world as the tiger's habitat is wanted to sustain the ever growing population of man.

The tiger is the largest of the big cats. It is a strikingly beautiful and majestic animal; lithe, agile and graceful. More cunning than a lion and with an awesome strength, males and females look similar though males have longer, more prominent cheek whiskers. The stripes and markings on the tiger's face and body vary, no two tigers are the same. Their colour ranges from reddish orange to yellow ochre, with tigers living at high altitudes tending to be paler. Completely black tigers have been reported but never photographed and there is a group of white tigers at Rewa, India. Their stripes are black and white rather than the usual black and orange and their eyes are blue.

Tigers are generally nocturnal animals and lead secret, well hidden lives. They seem to prefer damp places such as river banks and reed beds and can often be found in thickets of bamboo and long grass at the edge of the jungle. Tigers appear to enjoy swimming and basking in shallow water but apparently do not like to get water in their eyes and often enter a stream or pond backwards to avoid being splashed.

Unlike lions, tigers hunt alone, stealthily stalking their prey at dusk or in the night. They have an unfortunate penchant for raiding herds of domestic cattle which naturally leads to conflict, especially in tiger reserves where the tigers are protected. Older females will sometimes develop a taste for human flesh and though many reports of attacks on

RIGHT: Collage: tigers bathing in a jungle pool.

LEFT: A stitched Tiger cut out from its background makes an effective page decoration. The tiger's stripes make it almost invisible against a background of tall grass or jungle.

humans are greatly exaggerated, some are true; one well-known man-eater from a place called Champawat killed 430 people. It is much more usual, however, for tigers to kill and eat other wild animals such as various species of deer and antelope, wild boar, buffalo and sometimes even bears.

Tigers live on their own and are normally only seen in pairs for a short time during the breeding season. It was thought that males took no part in family life but recently male tigers have been observed in Ranthambhore National Park spending time with females and their cubs and even playing and sharing food with them. Gestation is 102-105 days; usually two to five cubs are born, though it is rare for more than two to be raised. The cubs remain with their mother for three years while she teaches them to hunt.

There are now only three races or subspecies of tiger left and all three are on the endangered species list. They are the Siberian, Bengal and Sumatran tigers. Others, such as the Chinese, Javan or Malaysian tigers are all extinct. The last wild Persian tiger from Iran and the Caucasus died mid-way through this century.

The Siberian tiger lives in the vast, wild and largely uninhabited areas of Eastern Siberia. It is the largest cat in the world today with males growing to a length of 13 ft (4 m). Mature males weigh in excess of ¼ ton (250 kg) with a record breaking specimen weighing in at just over ⅓ ton (300 kg). Siberian tigers have longer and shaggier coats than Indian tigers as an adaptation to the low temperatures in which they live. They are to be found in only the wildest and most inaccessible places, in thick forests or on rocky outcrops and mountain sides. They can live above the snow line at altitudes up to 8,000 ft (2,500 m). Sadly it is believed that there are only about 200 Siberian tigers left in the wild today though it is difficult to count them accurately in such a desolate and wide-spread terrain.

Bengal tigers are about 10 ft (3 m) long, a third of which is tail. They are found throughout India and are the most numerous of the three remaining races of tiger with about 2,500 left in the wild. The last of the three races is the smallest; the Sumatran tiger is now very rare with only about 30 left in the wild.

Tigers have been bred quite successfully in captivity. In Britain, Siberian tigers have been born and reared at Marwell Zoological Park in Hampshire and the largest breeding colony of captive tigers in the world is at John Aspinall's zoo, Howletts.

RIGHT: A Tiger worked on a yellow (C3) background has been framed in maple and then tiger stripes have been added to the frame with a black permanent marker pen.

1   2   3   4   5   6   7   8   9   10   11

WOOL COLOURS AND QUANTITIES

The quantities listed below are the numbers of yards of Elizabeth Bradley wool needed to work a piece measuring 160 stitches by 160 stitches on 10 mesh interlock canvas using cross stitch.

Colours used:

11 plus one background colour

The background colour of the Tiger shown on page 71 is yellow (C3).

Number on chart key	Elizabeth Bradley wool colours	Quantity (yards)
1	C5	13
2	C6	6
3	C7	20
4	C8	14
5	D9	12
6	D11	13
7	F3	10
8	G10	30
9	I6	25
10	I9	22
11	J7	24

Background quantity for a piece measuring 160 stitches by 160 stitches: 250 yards.

The Tiger chart

This Tiger chart is one of my more naive designs. It is reminiscent of both the early nineteenth-century woodcuts of tigers and of the many needlework pictures that were based on them. Most of these handsome and highly collectible embroidered tigers were worked in long and short stitch rather than in Berlin woolwork. This design was actually first painted about ten years ago when I had just started producing needlework kits rather than selling antique samplers and embroidery. It was originally intended to be one of the 12 designs of the Victorian Animal Series but I finally decided to use a lion and an elephant instead. The inclusion of the tiger would have made one too many naive style animals. I am very pleased to be able to publish it at long last and hope that those of you who have already embroidered the other 12 animals might like to add the tiger to your collection. It looks splendid on most background colours except perhaps black as its stripes, being a very dark brown, do not show up well against the black wool.

CHAPTER FIVE

Animal Worlds

Six Animal Habitats

The world or habitat of an animal is the place in which it lives and to which it is best suited. It does not exist there in isolation but is part of a group of associated plants and animals which form a distinct living community. Rainforest, moorland and tundra are all examples of types of habitat, each occurring due to a particular combination of physical conditions. The same habitat can be found in many different parts of the world and it is interesting to see how the same or similar species have developed in each independently. For instance, many large grazing mammals living on grassy plains have developed hooves so as to be able to run fast enough to escape from predators. Their young also have had to become adapted to the prevailing conditions, they would soon be eaten if they were as helpless as many new-born mammals and so the foals of antelopes and horses, for example, can stand and run almost from birth.

The life in any habitat is a finely balanced mixture of species which is only too easily damaged. Sometimes this happens unwittingly because not enough is known about them. Huge habitats such as the rainforest or the Poles are inaccessible and difficult to study whereas others such as a meadow, are more compact. By looking at such areas we can learn general rules that apply to all habitats and help us to understand them.

The six designs in this chapter are like windows looking into small intimate scenes in particular animal worlds. Rockpool and Trout Stream show life underwater; River Bank views some of the plants and animals found on and around the banks of a river; Moorland has its own set of highly specialized plants and animals, some of which are shown, and Harvest Field is a section through a somewhat old-fashioned and weedy cornfield. Vegetable Garden is rather an indulgence; it is a manmade habitat and I have included it among the other more classic environments because I wanted to feature a guinea pig and pet rabbit in this book and a garden habitat seemed the perfect place for them.

A great variety of animals and plants is shown in each design, each typical of that particular habitat. In order to achieve an interesting picture and to show each species so that it is easily recognizable, the scale had to be quite large. Some highly desirable animals like foxes, badgers and deer were too big to be featured in the foreground of a design and could only be shown in the distance so as to reduce them to a suitable size.

These habitat designs all look rather complicated and difficult to work. In actual fact, although intricate they are surprisingly easy to stitch, each block of colour is quite large and I have tried to avoid unnecessary shading. If you have enjoyed working the six designs featured here and would like to add to your collection then you might like to try a further four. These four are available as full kits only, they are Hedgerow, Woodland, Meadow and Duckpond.

PREVIOUS PAGE: A selection of the animal world designs nestle among ivy fronds.

RIGHT: Collage: viewed from underwater, rockpools, like reefs, can be extremely colourful places.

Rockpool

A rockpool is one of the most colourful and rewarding habitats to study. It is a magical, separate world teeming with animals and plants all living together in a small, enclosed pool of water resembling a natural aquarium. Many rockpools are only submerged at high tide and being shallow, isolated bodies of water, conditions in them vary from the open sea. There is much more light, temperature changes are more extreme and heavy rain can change salinity. Rockpools lower down the shore are under water for a longer period of time and so suffer fewer variations, they tend to be richer in terms of the number and diversity of species they support.

This rockpool contains a selection of the plants and animals that might typically be found there. Algae and sponges make brilliant patches of colour on the rocks. Weeds grow from the edges of the pool hanging in thick, waving curtains in which a prawn, two small fish and an edible crab can hide from marauding seagulls. Molluscs such as barnacles, limpets, top shells and mussels cling firmly in the crevices of the rocks hiding from a starfish whose muscular arms can detach most shells from their anchorages. Brightly coloured beadlet and opelet anemones open like flowers when left undisturbed and use their stinging tentacles to deter would-be predators. Brown, toothed wrack seaweed surrounds the picture and a cockle shell, attached to bright green sea lettuce, decorates each corner of the design.

WOOL COLOURS AND QUANTITIES

The quantities listed below are the numbers of yards of Elizabeth Bradley wool needed to work a piece measuring 160 stitches by 160 stitches on 10 mesh interlock canvas using cross stitch.

Colours used:
26 plus one background colour

Number on chart key	Elizabeth Bradley wool colours	Quantity (yards)
1	A6	13
2	A8	24
3	B4	33
4	B5	12
5	B7	7
6	C4	7
7	C6	10
8	C10	5
9	C11	16
10	E1	25
11	E2	21
12	E4	9
13	E6	33
14	E9	38
15	G10	10
16	H2	12
17	H3	19
18	H5	24
19	J3	10
20	J5	20
21	J10	28
22	J6	9
23	L1	58
24	M1	11
25	N9	12
26	N10	11

Background quantity for a piece measuring 160 stitches by 160 stitches: 90 yards.

THE ROCKPOOL'S CONTENTS

Acorn Barnacle *Semibalanus balanoides* Beadlet Anemone *Actinia equina* Black Goby *Gobius niger* Common Mussel *Mytilus edulis* Common Prawn *Leander serratus* Common Starfish *Asterias rubens* Corkwing Wrasse *Crenilabrus melops* Edible Cockle *Cerastoderma edule* Edible Crab *Cancer pagur* Irish Moss Seaweed *Chondrus crispus* Opelet Anemone *Anemonia sulcata* Painted Top Shell *Calliostoma zizyphinum* Purple Laver *Porphyra umbilicalis* Red Seaweeds *Laurencia pinnatifida, Membranoptera alata, Odonthalia dentata* Red Sponge *Hymeniacidon perleve* Sea Lettuce *Ulva lactuca* Toothed Wrack *Fucus serratus (border)* Tortoiseshell Limpet *Acmaea tessulata*

1   2   3   4   5   6   7   8   9   10   11   12   13   14   15   16   17   18   19   20   21   22   23   24   25   26

Harvest Field

Little of the land mass of Europe remains unaffected by its human inhabitants except perhaps the high mountain tops or the wildest and most inaccessible parts of the coast. Man has created the landscape that exists there today largely by his methods of farming and most of the habitats found in Europe are modified by agriculture to some degree. A modern wheat field is not a very natural environment. The sheltering hedges have probably been removed and the now large and featureless field will have been kept efficiently clear of weeds by the use of cleaned seed and selective weed killers.

In spite of modern methods of cultivation, a corn field can still support quite a rich variety of flora and fauna. In spring, the young wheat provides food for birds, mammals and insects. Rabbits, hares and deer nibble at the green shoots alongside pheasants and partridges. Ground nesting birds such as lapwings and skylarks find insects to eat in the freshly turned earth and hide their nests among the growing wheat stalks. In summer, the harvest mouse is sometimes still able to rear its young among the full grown corn and in autumn, wood pigeons gorge themselves on the grain before the stubble is ploughed in.

Many of the colourful flowers once closely associated with cornfields are now rare, existing only around the margins of the field where they escape spraying. The association of these plants with man can be traced back to prehistoric times. It is thought that their seeds were brought over from the Continent by British ancestors thousands of years ago,

they came mixed in with the grains of seed wheat and barley. Their flowers flourished among the corn and their seeds were ploughed in again each autumn.

It is sad not to have colourful and flowery cornfields anymore but apparently bread tastes better without at least some of their seeds. Corncockle seeds, for example, taint the flour, making it unpalatable and even mildly poisonous. On the other hand, poppy seeds scattered on top of a loaf of bread enhance its taste and in spite of all efforts to eradicate it, the poppy is alive and well in many cornfields. The corn poppy is a tenacious weed, each plant producing up to 17,000 seeds a year. These tiny seeds can remain dormant for up to 100 years and often a field red with poppies is indicative of it being disturbed or newly ploughed, causing thousands of dormant seeds to be brought to the surface.

The Harvest Field design

This needlework shows many traditional cornfield flowers growing in the grassy margin of a wheat field, while a brown hare sits motionless and alert with the ripe corn as a backdrop. The hare is a shy animal with powerful hind limbs, long sensitive ears with distinctive black tips and sharp eyes. It can run extremely fast and uses its good hearing and eyesight to give plenty of warning of approaching predators. It is mainly active at night or at dusk spending the daylight hours motionless in a shallow depression in the soil called a form. It feeds on leaves, buds, roots and berries. Hares live

LEFT: Rockpool (see pages 78-80) worked on a black (G11) background.

solitary lives making their exuberant courtship behaviour seem all the more extraordinary. Soon after the shortest day they gather together and dance, chasing each other, leaping into the air and boxing. I have seen hares dance on the salt marshes in Norfolk, their leaping shapes silhouetted black against the evening sky. It was a magical and unforgettable sight.

Above the watchful hare in the design is a pair of tiny and agile harvest mice. Harvest mice find it difficult to live in modern wheat fields and so, like these two, most of them have moved to the margins or into hedgerows and reed beds. They build distinctive tennis ball-sized nests woven from grass stems. First they build a supporting hammock from the living grass leaves and this is then used to support the other

plant debris and leaves that makes up the bulk of the nest. The living part of the nest remains green and helps to camouflage it.

The third animal in this picture is a sulphur yellow brimstone butterfly. It is a common species and is the first and last butterfly to be seen each year. It is often seen in cornfields as it searches for nectar in the wild flowers along their edges. The picture is edged with a border of corn cleavers and there is a corn marigold flower in each corner.

WOOL COLOURS AND QUANTITIES

The quantities listed below are the numbers of yards of Elizabeth Bradley wool needed to work a piece measuring 160 stitches by 160 stitches on 10 mesh interlock canvas using cross stitch.

Colours used:
29 plus one background colour

Number on chart key	Elizabeth Bradley wool colours	Quantity (yards)
1	A5	3
2	A8	10
3	B3	11
4	B11	11
5	C2	12
6	C3	27
7	C5	19
8	D2	19
9	D6	12
10	D7	17
11	D10	9
12	E5	17
13	E7	38
14	F2	14
15	F4	11
16	F10	32
17	G8	5
18	G10	4
19	I1	8
20	I3	17
21	I4	17
22	I8	16
23	J6	38
24	J9	14
25	J10	51
26	J11	17
27	L1	18
28	L10	4
29	N10	9

Background quantity for a piece measuring 160 stitches by 160 stitches: 90 yards.

1   2   3   4   5   6   7   8   9   10   11   12   13   14   15   16   17   18   19   20   21   22   23   24   25   26   27   28   29

ABOVE: *Harvest Field worked on a red (B8) background.*
RIGHT: *Collage: a harvested field leaves hares and harvest mice dangerously exposed to predators.*
They have to seek shelter elsewhere until the corn grows again.

Moorland

The mountains in the background of this chart are coloured greyish purple because they are covered with great carpets of heather in full flower. Moorland is typically high, wet and windy and its most obvious feature is the many species of heather that grow there. Heather tolerates having its roots immersed in wet peat; a coarse, acid soil which acts rather like a sponge retaining rain water all year round. Heather has narrow, leathery leaves to minimize water loss because the water around its roots is frozen and so unavailable for much of the year; the wind howling across the moor in winter will also dry out and even scorch any plant that is not adapted to withstand it. The heather shown to the right of this design is the large flowered bell heather.

Which plants grow where on a moor is largely determined by the degree of drainage. Where the soil is totally water-logged, areas of bog become established allowing plants such as the sundew (centre of design) and the bog violet or butterwort (foreground of design) to flourish. Cowberry (right side of design) will grow on the edge of boggy areas while bilberries (whose matt, purple berries can be seen edging the picture), need better drainage to thrive. Over to the right is a patch of gorse which grows on lower slopes of the hillsides. In contrast, the snow gentians (painted in each corner of the design), thrive at the upper reaches of the moorland world on the snow line.

Many people will probably never have seen the fascinating and distinctive moorland bird in the centre of this chart. It is a black grouse or blackcock and is found living on the edges of moor or heath near trees. The males have dramatic blue-black plumage with white feathers on the wings and under the tail. The female, or greyhen, is a brown-ish, well camouflaged bird. Every dawn, except when they are moulting, black grouse gather in large groups to display at favoured traditional sites called leks. Males fluff up their white undertail feathers and raise their lyre shaped tails, all the while cooing in a regular repeating pattern. The males strut and bustle about while the inconspicuous females watch in apparent admiration.

Below the grouse is an adder coiled up basking in the sun on a patch of sand. The adder is the most widely distributed snake in Britain and the only one that is poisonous. Adders are distinctively marked with a dark zigzag all the way down their backs and a V for Viper on their heads. Although they are timid snakes they will bite man and cattle if trodden on or caught unawares. The bite is not fatal but medical treatment should be sought. Their normal prey is lizards, frogs, toads, mice and voles which they hunt by stealth, creeping up on them and killing them with a poisonous bite, the venom injected by means of hollow, ringed fangs. If the prey is not immediately immobilized then the adder will trail it using the heat sensors on its snout.

Above the adder is a large black slug which is a common sight in upland pastures, as are clouds of biting blackflies. Above the gorse, a Scotch Argus butterfly flutters in the sun; this species is a remnant from the last

RIGHT: Moorland worked on a red (B8) background.

OVERLEAF: Collage: wild, wet moorland is home to a surprisingly large number of animals.

1 2 3 4 5 6 7 8 9 10 11 12 13 14 15 16 17 18 19 20 21 22 23 24 25 26

WOOL COLOURS AND QUANTITIES

The quantities listed below are the numbers of yards of Elizabeth Bradley wool needed to work a piece measuring 160 stitches by 160 stitches on 10 mesh interlock canvas using cross stitch.

Colours used:

26 plus one background colour

Number on chart key	Elizabeth Bradley wool colours	Quantity (yards)
1	A3	6
2	B11	6
3	C5	13
4	D5	17
5	D9	18
6	F7	8
7	F9	18
8	F3	9
9	G8	33
10	G10	23
11	H2	12
12	H3	21
13	H5	16
14	I1	16
15	I3	26
16	I5	20
17	J6	25
18	J8	28
19	J11	11
20	K7	21
21	L1	30
22	M8	17
23	L11	18
24	N1	18
25	N8	22
26	N5	6

Background quantity for a piece measuring 160 stitches by 160 stitches: 90 yards.

ice age, having been around on the high moors in Scotland for the last 10,000 years. They are brown butterflies with orange spots or eyes on the wings, and they fly when it is sunny and rest in the grass in dull weather. Lower down, in the gorse bush itself, are a pair of clouded buff tiger moths which can be seen on the moors during June and July when they lay their eggs on bell heather. The Emperor moth is another insect whose young feed on heather. It is the only native British member of the silkworm family though sadly its cocoons are not suitable for silk production. While the female flies only at night, the male is out in the daytime too, and it is thought that the large false eyes on the wings may help to deter potential bird predators.

Last of all the insects in this design are the four brilliantly coloured, green tiger beetles, one in each corner. This beetle can run faster than any other British insect and is a ferocious predator, galloping after other insects in order to capture and eat them.

Trout Stream

Most streams are born high up on hill and mountain sides; clean, clear water gushes out from among the rocks and races downwards. If the ground is steep, the stream is a rushing torrent while in the valleys it flows slower and more sinuously, forming pools and stretches of gently moving water rich with weed and fish.

A stream is a more complicated habitat than a rockpool, there are more factors to consider. For instance, the animals that live there must prevent themselves from being swept away by the current. Fish can maintain their position by active swimming but other smaller animals have to anchor themselves or stay sheltered among the weeds. Food is constantly on the move too. Phytoplankton drifts with the stream while nutritious plant and animal detritus is carried ever downstream towards the sea. At least algae remains stationary and can be grazed as it grows on stones and water weed.

The Trout Stream design

This needlework gives some idea of the complexity and richness of an underwater stream environment. The central characters are the four species of fish, they are all predators, eating not only other animals but each other. A European brown trout is in the centre, swimming upwards to grab a caddis-fly larvae. Brown trout are difficult to see from above being greyish brown in colour with a lighter belly. They are also speckled all over with many red, yellow and black spots. Young trout eat mainly larvae while older fish eat winged insects, fresh water shrimps and smaller fish. They themselves are eaten by larger trout, otters, mink, shrews, herons, pike and, of course, man.

To the right of the trout are three minnows, they are pretty, darting fish often living in shoals of up to a hundred strong. They have cylindrical bodies about 4 ins (10 cms) long, silvery or brownish grey marked with dark bars. During the spawning season in May they develop a pink belly like the minnows shown here. They live in the deeper parts of small brooks and streams, preferring a gravelly bottom to silty mud.

Below the trout are a couple of tiddlers, which are the tiny fish often caught by small boys with a line and a bent pin. Tiddlers are actually three-spined sticklebacks, small carnivorous fish, about 3-4 ins (7.5-10 cms) long that eat crustaceans, water fleas, invertebrates, worms, larvae and fish eggs.

Sticklebacks have most unusual and elaborate breeding habits. First of all the male develops a red underbelly, he then takes over a territory at the bottom of the stream and drives out all the other male sticklebacks. In the centre of this territory he builds a nest of small pieces of plant material glued together with a sticky secretion from his kidneys. Finally, he persuades a succession of females to enter his nest. They are attracted by his distinctive zigzag dance and once enticed into the nest can be persuaded to lay eggs by a brisk nudge in the side and trembling encouragement. The eggs are then fertilized by his secreting a cloud of sperm or milt over them. Before the eggs hatch, the male aerates them by fanning with his fins.

RIGHT: *Trout Stream worked on a red (B8) background.*

Hovering above the male stickleback's tail in the design is another carnivore, the voracious perch with its plump, yellowish tinged body striped with dark bars and well-developed, fan-like fins. Perfectly camouflaged, it will lurk among the weeds until ready to dash out and grab its prey. The perch is a cannibal, often biting and damaging the tails of smaller perch before swallowing them head first.

The two other vertebrates in the design are both amphibians. The frog on the right and the newt on the left will spend much of their time on land but will always return to water to spawn. Frogs lay their eggs in glutinous masses while newts produce ribbons of eggs which become entwined among the water weeds. Both kinds of eggs hatch into tadpoles.

To the left of the design, a great diving beetle clings to the flowering stems of pipewort while a great ramshorn snail climbs up the thick fleshy stem of a white water lily with its arum shaped underwater leaves. Anyone who has kept tropical fish will recognize the red twisting threads of the sludge or tubifex worm anchored in their muddy cone-like homes. Finally, there

are two crustaceans, the larger one a crayfish which is hiding beneath a clump of tapegrass while near the frog a tiny water shrimp hangs almost transparent in the water. The picture is framed by the neat regular fronds of Canadian pondweed and a three-petalled arrowhead flower adorns each corner.

RIGHT: An old stick back elbow chair has been made more comfortable with pads made from Trout Stream and Rock Pool pieces. The pads have been attached by wide tapes made from fine green woollen cloth.

WOOL COLOURS AND QUANTITIES

The quantities listed below are the numbers of yards of Elizabeth Bradley wool needed to work a piece measuring 160 stitches by 160 stitches on 10 mesh interlock canvas using cross stitch.

Colours used:
27 plus one background colour

Number on chart key	Elizabeth Bradley wool colours	Quantity (yards)
1	B3	3
2	B7	10
3	C1	11
4	C2	11
5	C6	7
6	C10	2
7	C11	7
8	D10	7
9	E4	18
10	F1	14
11	F7	25
12	G10	5
13	H1	8
14	H3	17
15	H5	25
16	I1	19
17	I2	17
18	I4	14
19	J6	43
20	J8	16
21	J10	11
22	J11	18
23	K9	20
24	K10	16
25	K11	8
26	L1	75
27	N11	3

Background quantity for a piece measuring 160 stitches by 160 stitches: 90 yards.

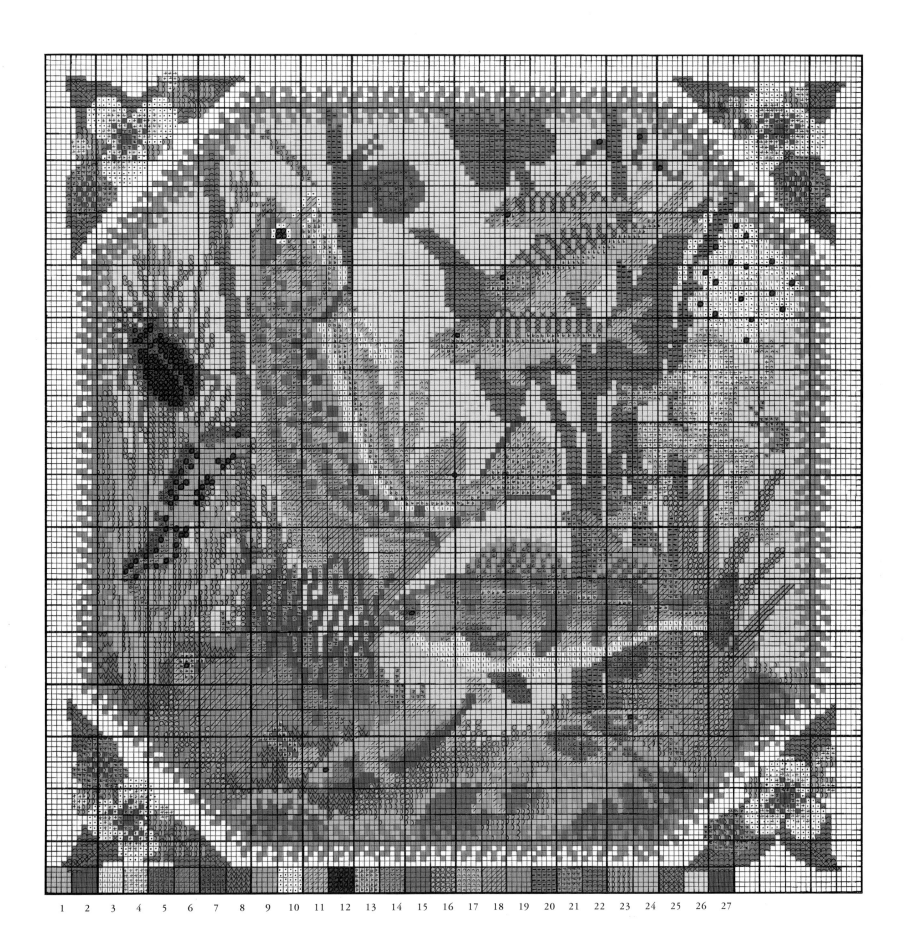

1   2   3   4   5   6   7   8   9   10   11   12   13   14   15   16   17   18   19   20   21   22   23   24   25   26   27

River Bank

Quiet river banks in the countryside are some of the most unspoilt and important of habitats. The higher reaches of many rivers are still privately owned and renting out stretches along their banks for fishing is a valuable source of income for landowners. Fishing is a very popular hobby whether it is game fishing for salmon and trout or coarse fishing for bream, tench, roach, perch and pike. Successful fishing needs peace and quiet, unpolluted water and an undisturbed river, so in this habitat at least, the interests of man and wildlife coincide.

Although a river bank can be an enchanting and peaceful place, there is plenty of activity if you know what to look out for. Sometimes one sees a flash of blue as a kingfisher speeds past or more rarely a webbed otter footprint in the mud. Dragon- and damselflies with brilliant iridescent wings often flit above the surface of the water. Both the banded demoiselle damselfly with its blue blotched wings and the emperor dragonfly are large insects, powerful fliers that spend their brief lives dashing to and fro along the river catching small airborne insects. The young dragonflies, or nymphs, live underwater. They moult repeatedly as they grow until eventually they are big enough to climb up a reed or grass stalk to the surface. Once above water they shed their last skin, shake out their new wings to dry and fly, usually emerging in the early morning or at dusk. Nocturnal moths also appear when the light fades. A boldly patterned, cream spotted, tiger moth can be seen at each corner of the design and two cream-bordered,

sweetpea moths flutter in the centre.

Vegetation grows lush and luxuriant at the margin of the river bank. In the deep water behind the otter grow tall stands of stately bulrush, cheerful clumps of yellow iris and spikes of purple loosestrife. In the foreground, bur-weed and creeping yellow cress grow in the shallows while soft blue water forget-me-nots and the white flowers of water crowfoot add a touch of colour to the muddy banks.

Otters are the largest member of the weasel family and the one in the centre of this design sits sunning himself on a rock while surveying his domain. They are inhabitants of clear, unpolluted streams where they feed mainly on a diet of slow moving fish with crayfish, frogs, birds, ducks and moorhens on the side. Although far less numerous than before, they are still a very widespread carnivore. Their shape is streamlined and their feet webbed, they swim with grace and agility and with their large lungs can stay underwater for up to four minutes. Their eyes and nostrils are on top of the head so they can see and breathe even when the rest of their body is submerged. They have long sensitive vibrissae to help them find their way underwater and a thick, water-repellent coat and layer of subcutaneous fat keeps them warm and dry.

A kingfisher, a most exotic looking bird, is the other star of this design. Its feathers are brilliantly coloured to deter predators and it has a sharp beak for spearing fish. It is a surprisingly small bird, only 6½ ins (16.5 cms) long and is shy of man so that

THE CONTENTS OF THE
RIVER BANK

Banded Demoiselle
Agrion splendens

Bulrush
Typha latifolia

Cream-bordered Green Pea Moth
Earias clorana

Cream Spot Tiger Moth
Arctia villica

Creeping Yellow Cress
Rorippa sylvestris (border and design)

Emperor Dragonfly
Anax imperator

Kingfisher
Alcedo atthis

Marsh Marigold
Caltha palustris (leaves in corners)

Otter
Lutra lutra

Purple Loosestrife
Lythrum salicaria

Unbranched Burweed
Sparganium simplex

Water Crowfoot
Ranunculus fluitans

Water Forget-me-not
Myosotis scorpioides

Yellow Iris
Iris pseudacorus

RIGHT: River Bank worked on a red (B8) background.

1 2 3 4 5 6 7 8 9 10 11 12 13 14 15 16 17 18 19 20 21 22 23

WOOL COLOURS AND QUANTITIES

The quantities listed below are the numbers of yards of Elizabeth Bradley wool needed to work a piece measuring 160 stitches by 160 stitches on 10 mesh interlock canvas using cross stitch.

Colours used:

23 plus one background colour

Number on chart key	Elizabeth Bradley wool colours	Quantity (yards)
1	A5	4
2	C4	6
3	C7	13
4	C8	13
5	D4	34
6	D9	23
7	F3	12
8	F5	14
9	F9	43
10	F11	47
11	G10	16
12	H3	18
13	H4	21
14	I1	21
15	I4	42
16	J6	15
17	J9	12
18	J10	13
19	J11	17
20	K5	20
21	L1	45
22	M1	10
23	M2	8

Background quantity for . piece measuring 160 stitches by 160 stitches: 90 yards.

RIGHT: Collage: a kingfisher and an otter fishing together.

often all that is ever seen of it is a flash of electric blue as it passes. Its timidity is deceptive because it is actually a highly territorial, aggressive and busy bird that is seldom still; it produces broods of young throughout the summer and is a very efficient fisherman, catching fish on four out of five dives. Like the kingfisher in this design, it can sometimes be seen hovering motionless above the water waiting to swoop on an unsuspecting fish.

The young are raised in burrows, up to 1 yd (1 m) long, that are dug by both the male and the female using their powerful bills and feet. The adult birds make the tunnel wide enough for them to fly straight into, even with a fish held in their bills. Each chick eats between 12 and 18 fish a day and they are fed in strict rotation. Kingfishers are very messy housekeepers and never clean their burrows, which become so smelly and slimy that the adults usually need a cleansing dive each time they emerge.

The tiger moths at each corner of the design sit on heart-shaped marsh marigold leaves and the frame enclosing the design is made up of the flowers and buds of the creeping yellow cress.

Vegetable Garden

Most of the plants found growing in a vegetable garden are destined for the table. It is a cultivated world, planted with a fruitful harvest in mind, though a few unwanted visitors do manage to flourish there in spite of every effort to evict them; these plants are called weeds. Although it is a contrived and artificial world, such a garden is a surprisingly rich habitat and acts as a haven for many wild species. While many birds and mammals, such as hedgehogs and squirrels, are encouraged to live there, life is not so rosy for insects and other invertebrates like greenfly, slugs and woodlice. Unless the gardener is a nature lover or a believer in organic gardening they are likely to be totally wiped out by regular doses of weed killer, insecticide and slug pellets.

The Vegetable Garden design

Robins and song thrushes are two favourite garden birds and an example of each can be seen perched on a couple of flower pots towards the top of the chart. Robins are often called the gardener's friend because they seem unafraid of man and will often perch nearby when digging is being done. Males and females look the same, both having neat brown bodies, beady black eyes and bright vermilion breast feathers. Most vegetable gardens have only one resident robin which guards its territory jealously. If another intrudes, it will first display its red breast and if this signal is ignored then the visitor will be forcibly ejected. In cold weather, the rules are relaxed slightly and sometimes several robins can be seen feeding together at a bird table.

Both birds nest in gardens but thrushes are far shyer birds, keeping out of sight and sometimes only giving away their presence by their distinctive song. They eat mainly worms and snails and have the unique habit of always cracking the snail shells on one particular and prominent stone in the garden called a thrush anvil. The ground around it becomes littered with broken shells which act as another indicator that a thrush is living in the vegetable garden.

Butterflies make charming and welcome visitors to the vegetable garden as they flutter about sipping nectar from the flowers. Their hungry caterpillars are less welcome. Those of the large white butterfly can devour a row of healthy cabbages or other brassicas in no time at all. Red admiral butterflies are a familiar sight in gardens and there is one resting on a leaf in each corner of the chart. Fortunately, these colourful butterflies lay their eggs on nettles and so pose no problems for gardeners. Adults are particularly partial to the nectar from Michaelmas daisies and buddleia and are not averse to feeding on rotting windfalls: they add a special charm to many vegetable gardens in autumn.

The snail climbing the flower pot would be wise to keep out of sight of the thrush on top though no doubt most gardeners would be pleased if it was seen and eaten. Snails do a lot of damage to certain plants and can be a major pest. Of the flowers and vegetables in this design they seem especially attracted to lettuces and cabbages, in my experience they tend to leave carrots, tomatoes, courgettes

LEFT: Vegetable Garden worked on a black (G11) background.

and chives alone. Lobelia and dandelions appear to be delectable on occasion but stone crop never. The design is framed by a border of box leaves, small clipped hedges of this evergreen shrub have been used to edge vegetable beds for centuries.

The aliens in the picture are the three pets in the foreground. They are sitting on a stone-flagged path with stone crop growing in the cracks and munching their way through a meal of a carrot, tomatoes and a cabbage leaf. The guinea pig on the right is a shy vegetarian from the grasslands of South America. Bred by the local populace as a source of meat and being easy to keep in captivity, they were carried by traders all over the world. Originally plain brown or black animals, they have been selectively bred to produce the many fancy varieties now available. Domesticated rabbits too come in all shapes and sizes, the variety pictured here is a bi-coloured Dutch. The third member of the trio is a small tortoise from the southern Mediterranean area. Thousands of these reptiles were brought to Britain as pets, only to die in our colder and wetter climate, their import is restricted nowadays to protect stocks in the wild.

WOOL COLOURS AND QUANTITIES

The quantities listed below are the numbers of yards of Elizabeth Bradley wool needed to work a piece measuring 160 stitches by 160 stitches on 10 mesh interlock canvas using cross stitch.

Colours used:
28 plus one background colour

Number on chart key	Elizabeth Bradley wool colours	Quantity (yards)
1	B4	18
2	B5	31
3	B9	7
4	B10	7
5	C7	11
6	C8	4
7	D4	8
8	D7	3
9	E1	13
10	E5	15
11	F3	26
12	F4	8
13	F6	18
14	F7	16
15	F9	17
16	F11	20
17	G10	26
18	H7	13
19	H8	26
20	H9	13
21	I1	20
22	I4	17
23	J6	63
24	J8	58
25	J10	26
26	K7	11
27	L1	21
28	M3	3

Background quantity for a piece measuring 160 stitches by 160 stitches: 90 yards.

OVERLEAF: Collage: tame rabbits and guinea pigs nibble the vegetables and flowers in this sunny summer garden.

1 2 3 4 5 6 7 8 9 10 11 12 13 14 15 16 17 18 19 20 21 22 23 24 25 26 27 28

Ivy Leaf Border

Ivy growing up a wall or around a window arranges itself naturally into a border as the leaves grow already suitably placed along a central stem. Uncultivated country ivy has plain dark green leaves relieved by a distinct pattern of paler veins fanning out from the base of each tri-lobed leaf. Ivy borders featuring such leaves are suitable for edging almost any type of central design. They make perfect frames for needlework whether it is worked in classical or Victorian style or based on natural history or flowers.

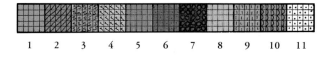

THIS PAGE AND OPPOSITE: Two rows of squares have been left blank on both of these charts. The blank squares that occur between the outer two rows, yellow ochre (C6) and grass green (J6), and the four rows of darker green (J8), are to indicate a delay in working. The two outermost rows are worked AFTER the carpet has been joined together. Note: Please read the instructions on page 112 for Making and Attaching the Border BEFORE starting to stitch these border sections.

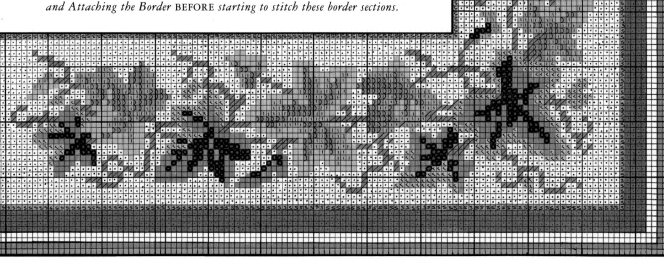

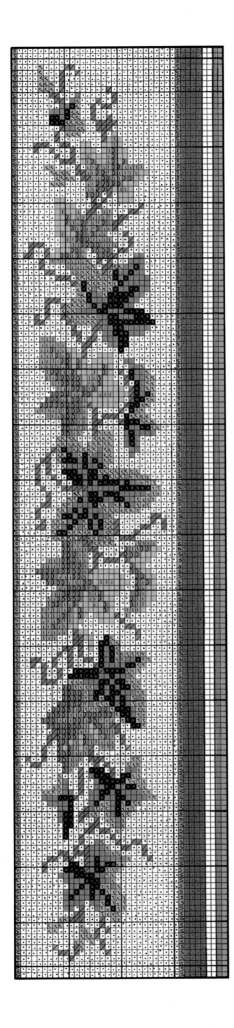

The Ivy pattern on each section of the border is separate and distinct, it does not carry on continuously from one piece to the next. Instead, there is a gap of a few rows of plain background between each side and corner section. These rows have been left unpatterned deliberately to make this border easier to join and more adaptable to use.

This border is designed to edge squares of needlework that measure 160 stitches by 160 stitches. The number of rows of plain background can be increased if larger central squares are required, and decreased if the pieces in the centre are smaller than the standard 160 stitches by 160 stitches. It works on exactly the same principal as the Ribbon and Bow Border produced by Elizabeth Bradley Designs Ltd and the instructions below are a slightly modified version of those issued with that kit.

The carpet on page 111 has been made with six central squares while the square one on page 163 has nine panels. The central squares of such a carpet are made separately and then sewn together and edged with the border. The pieces are joined by overlapping the edges of the canvases and then stitching through both layers.

Making a carpet with the Ivy Leaf Border

Please read the following instructions very carefully before starting your carpet.

- All the central squares of a carpet should measure 160 stitches by 160 stitches.
- Each of the squares in a carpet should be worked with the same background colour and the background of the border should be worked to match.
- Cross stitch is the most suitable stitch to use throughout. It produces thick square pieces of needlework with no distortion in shape.

WOOL COLOURS AND QUANTITIES

The quantities listed below are the numbers of yards of Elizabeth Bradley wool needed to work the various components of the Ivy Leaf Border and to join and edge a six-panel carpet. The border and carpet squares are worked on 10 mesh interlock canvas using cross stitch.

Colours used:
11 including one background colour

The background colour of the border of the six-panel carpet shown on page 111 is black (G11) and the background colour of the border of the nine-panel carpet shown on page 163 is red (B8).

Number on chart key	Elizabeth Bradley wool colours	Quantity A corner	A side piece
1	C6	-	-
2	D10	13	9
3	I4	10	9
4	J4	12	9
5	J6	11	10
6	J8	21	16
7	K6	9	9
8	K3	10	9
9	K5	10	9
10	K11	10	9
11	G11	63	58

Key number 11
is the background colour.

Wool colours and quantities to join and edge a six-panel carpet.

Number on chart key	Elizabeth Bradley wool colours	Quantity (yards)
1	C6	160
3	I4	84
5	J6	130
6	J8	440

Sewing horizontal and vertical joints

Horizontal joints run parallel to the rows of stitches in the central squares. Stitches should be worked as shown in the diagram on page 158, with each cross stitch being worked in the same direction as all the other cross stitches in the carpet. Vertical joints attach the side of one piece of needlework to the side of the next, they run across the rows of stitches in the central squares and are at right angles to them. The two pieces can be joined by working short rows of four stitches all the way up the joint as is shown in diagram 1.

An easier alternative is to turn the vertical joint on its side and work rows of stitches along its length. This method will only work, however, if the stitch is reversed. If worked normally, each stitch will run in the opposite direction to the others in the carpet when the joined section is returned to the upright position. This would look unsightly and spoil the look of the work. Reversed cross stitches are achieved by working the stitches upside down, starting at the top of each stitch and completing it at the top, rather than as usual, starting and completing it at the bottom.

Joining the central section of the carpet

Each square in the central section of the carpet is separated from the next by a band of eight rows of stitches. The first two rows, one yellow ochre (C6) and the other grass green (J6) must be worked around each square separately before joining. The four

oak-leaf green (J8) rows between them actually join the squares together and are worked through both pieces of canvas when they have been overlapped.

The technique of reversing stitches, as already described, is useful for working these first two single rows of stitches. Start stitching at the bottom right-hand corner of the square using normal cross stitch all along the row until the corner is reached. Turn the corner and immediately reverse the stitch before working up the left-hand side of the piece. The top row can then be worked as normal. Reverse the stitch again for working down the right-hand side of the square back to the starting point.

Before working the two rows of stitches, CHECK CAREFULLY that the square measures exactly 160 stitches by 160 stitches. If it does not, then the carpet will not join up properly. If the finished pieces need stretching or blocking this should be done before joining them together.

Having stitched the two edging rows, decide on the arrangement of the squares of the carpet. The six-panel carpet overleaf is made up of three pairs of needlework squares. To duplicate the arrangement, first join River Bank to Vegetable Garden, then Moorland to Rockpool and last Trout Stream to Harvest Field. The first pair of joined squares should then be joined to the one below it and the last pair to the joined four squares above it in the carpet. In the case of the nine-panel carpet on page 163, follow the same principal, joining together each trio of squares before attaching them to the trios below.

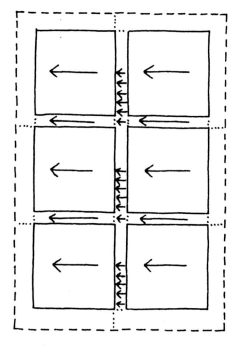

Diagram 1: The arrows show the direction of stitching in the central squares and in the rows that join them together.

RIGHT: Collage: a wreath of ivy, apples and birds.

Joining together two pieces

• Overlap the unworked canvas of the two pieces being joined, leaving a gap of four threads (three holes) between the edges of the pieces.

• Tack the layers of canvas in place carefully before sewing the joining rows of cross stitch. 'T'-shaped tacks work best and they should be stitched at each end of a joint and then at regular intervals, every 2 or 3 ins (5 or 7.5 cms) along it.

• Leave the pieces of canvas untrimmed and work three of the four joining rows.

• Trim the canvas of the top piece back to the fourth thread, cutting as near as possible to the fifth thread so that little ends of cut canvas are left sticking out – these will help to prevent thread four from unravelling. To make absolutely sure that this does not happen it is best to trim the canvas as you go along, cutting just a few inches (centimetres) ahead of where you are sewing and leaving the rest untrimmed.

• As you stitch the fourth and final row, snip off the little ends of canvas as you come to them. If they are not removed at this stage they will show afterwards as a row of little white dots along the join.

• Where four squares join, the stitching will be through four pieces of canvas. Tack this section in place very carefully and be very gentle with the canvas at this point. If the canvas should unravel it will be more difficult to achieve a perfect join.

• The canvas sticking out at the back after joining can be trimmed up to the stitching line leaving a practically invisible join back and front.

• It takes practice to make a perfect join. It is likely that the work will probably seem awkward and difficult to handle at first. With perseverance, however, this joining technique becomes easier and is a very useful technique for attaching two or more pieces of canvas together.

Making and attaching the border

The border is made up of four corner sections and a variable number of side sections, depending on the size of the carpet (see digram 2). For this six-square carpet, six side sections will be needed and each section is joined to the next with four rows of stitching. **To make the join, leave the last two rows at the end of each border section unworked.** Overlap the canvas and tack it in place as described above and then stitch the four missing rows of the border through the double layer of canvas.

The border sections can be made separately and then joined together at the end when they are all complete, or they can be joined as the work progresses in a continuous and complete border.

When stitching the border pieces (both corners and side sections), stitch only the pale green (I4) row of stitches on the inside edge. The border is then attached to the joined central squares by using exactly the same method as before with the four oak-leaf green (J8) rows.

Diagram 2: To make a carpet with the Ivy Leaf border, four corner pieces are always necessary. The number of pairs of side sections that will be required depends on the size of carpet being made.

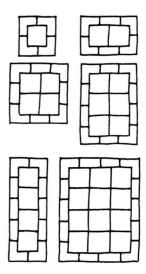

RIGHT: The carpet opposite has been made with six central squares surrounded by the Ivy Border. Both squares and border are worked on a black (G11) background.

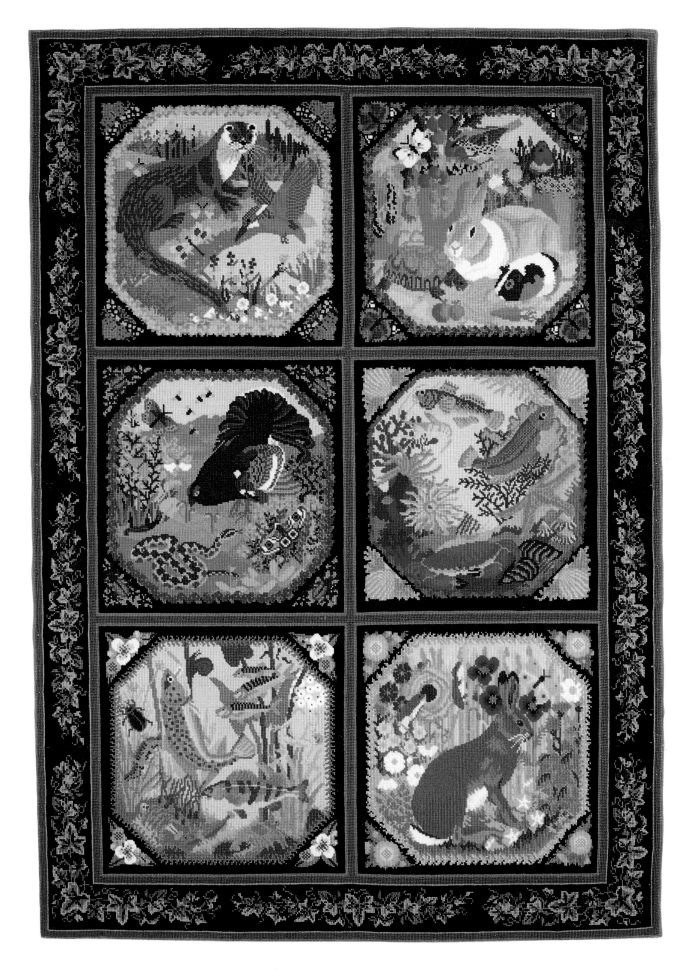

On the outside of the border sections, stitch the pale green (I4) row and the four oak-leaf green (J8) rows only. Leave the yellow ochre (C6) and grass green (J6) rows until later when the carpet has been joined together.

Be very careful to work all the border sections correctly or they will not fit around the joined central squares. Count and check constantly as the work progresses.

The direction of all the stitches in the border should match those in the central squares and so the stitching of the border sections must be planned according to the layout of the carpet.

If the pieces of canvas have a selvedge this should always be positioned on the right-hand side and the pieces – as usual – should be stitched from right to left (see materials and methods).

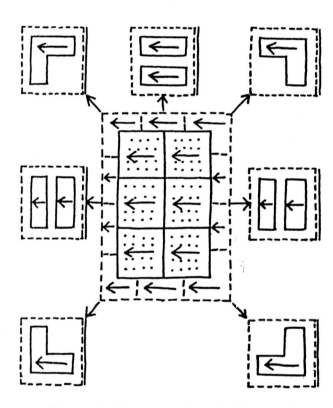

Diagram 3: The arrows show the direction of
stitching on the various sections that make up
the border of a six-square carpet.

Making a neat outside edge for the carpet

To finish off the carpet neatly:

• On the back of the carpet, trim any excess canvas at the joints. It can be trimmed right up to the stitching line if desired.

• Trim the canvas all around the carpet to a minimum of eight rows.

• Fold the canvas over at the edge leaving two threads showing at the front.

• Mitre the corners. To do this make a fold diagonally across the canvas, three threads out from the edge of the stitching. Fold the edges of the canvas over as before, leaving two threads showing at the front (see diagram 4).

• Work the grass green (J6) row of stitches through both layers of the folded canvas covering the first thread. There will be two threads left unworked on the fold. At the mitred corners, work the grass green (J6) row through four thicknesses of canvas where necessary.

• To make a neat bound edge, sew over the two threads with the yellow ochre (C6) wool. First stitch one way, over and over all the way around the carpet and then stitch back the other way.

Finishing off the back of the carpet

If the carpet is to be laid onto a stone or wooden floor then it should either be lined or tacked to an insulating pad of carpet felt placed between the carpet and the floor. Upholstery hessian makes a good traditional lining. To stop it from bagging, attach the hessian lightly to the back of the carpet with rows of tacking stitches.

If the carpet is to be laid onto a fitted carpet it is best left unlined as it will slip around less. Just hem or herringbone stitch hessian webbing or cotton tape to cover the cut edge of the folded canvas around the outside. The same tape can also be sewn over all the joints for added protection.

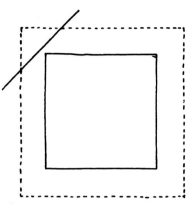

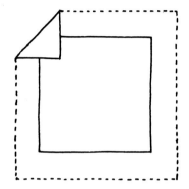

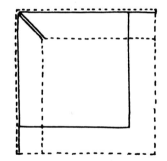

Diagram 4: Mitring the corners of a carpet.

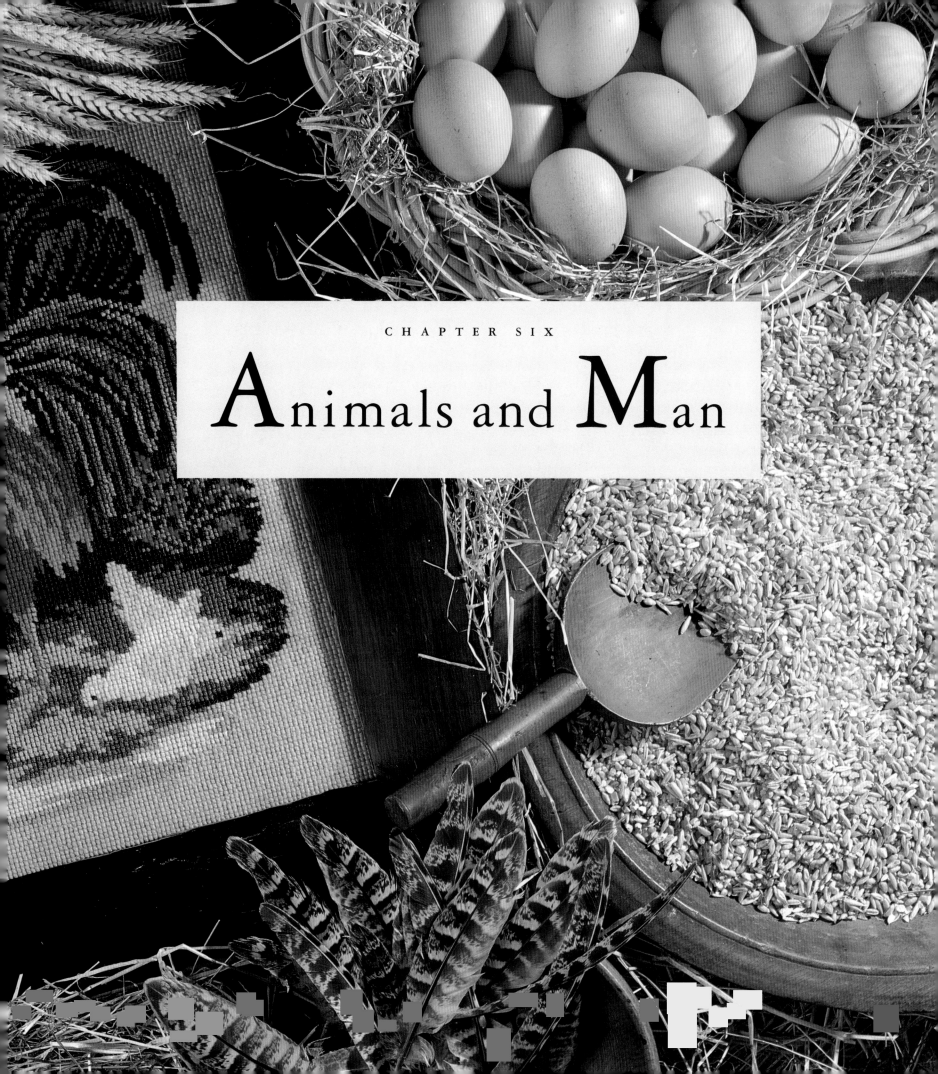

CHAPTER SIX

Animals and Man

Animals and Man

Since he settled down and became 'civilized', man has not only changed many aspects of his environment but has also managed to gradually alter the physical appearance of some of those animals that live closest to him. He has done this by means of selective breeding over the course of many centuries. In years gone by, the process happened naturally; not through any scientific plan but just because it seemed a sensible thing to do. Domestic animals which showed advantageous traits were bred from more frequently, causing gradual physical changes in a direction that was helpful to man.

The degree to which an animal's physical appearance can be altered can be seen at its most extreme in dogs. All dogs are descended from the smaller, southern strain of the grey wolf (*Canis lupus pallipes*), which still lives in India. The genetic heritage of such an animal is amazingly strong and in spite of profound physical differences, all canines are virtually the same physiologically and in their behaviour patterns. This can be readily observed at dog training classes. A young Pekingese or Chihuahua behaves much the same as a baby Alsation or Mastiff and no doubt a wolf cub brought up under the same conditions would display similar traits. This fidelity to heritage can be observed in all domesticated species – cattle, horses, chickens and pigs of whatever breed seem to stay pretty close in spirit to their wild ancestors.

Wild species of chickens and pigs were hunted by early man as a useful source of meat and were probably domesticated so that they could be used for food more conveniently. Fetching a hen from the hen run or a pig from the pig sty was considerably easier and more condusive to regular mealtimes than going off to find one in the forest.

Dogs and cats are not generally eaten by human beings but live with them in a mutually beneficial relationship. In return for being fed and housed, a dog gives uncritical companionship and an unqualified welcome to his master or mistress. Some breeds also work for their living and appear to enjoy doing so. Sheep dogs help farmers gather scattered sheep on inaccessible terrain. Other breeds act as guard dogs or assist the police. With special training, some dogs will sniff out drugs in luggage or cargo, guide blind people, retrieve game birds after they have been shot, pull sledges and find avalanche victims buried in the snow. All these activities can be related to a dog's natural instincts and lifestyle as one of a pack of social, hunting carnivores. Once the human master has established himself as dominant in the pack of two, the dog will be subservient to him and, in theory, amenable to his command.

Cats are more independent, with most wild species of cats being naturally solitary animals only forming pairs and family groups for the purpose of mating and kitten care. Their relationship with their owner can seem almost condescending in that they will happily accept food and a limited amount of petting from their humans, but the rest of the time is their own. Some are prepared to use their natural hunting instincts to be helpful by killing mice and rats around the house or farm. The songbirds that they also catch are a less welcome present. Cats do not train easily but seem to be adaptable and sensible creatures, apparently quite content to live their lives in comfortable human houses, being fed once or twice a day and coming and going at will through cat doors constructed for their convenience.

PREVIOUS PAGE:
Needlework chickens, corn, brown eggs, treen, baskets and hay combine to make a mellow rustic picture. The chickens are worked on a yellow (C3) background.

RIGHT:
Collage: a selection of animals that have been domesticated by man.

Marmalade Cat

Some people might argue that a cat (*Felis catus*) is man's best friend rather than a dog. Some homes house both species, but most people seem to be polarized into being either a cat fan or a dog lover, a third alternative group is neutral to both and really cannot understand why anyone would want to live with either of them. Cats have been domesticated for a far shorter time than dogs and so their physique and nature remains very close to wild cats. Selective breeding has concentrated on their fine, silky, fur coats rather than their shape.

There are 36 species of modern cat including lions, tigers, pumas, leopards, ocelot and lynx, to mention just a few. Several of the smaller species are wild cats and there has been much discussion over the years as to which of them was the ancestor of the domestic cat. Opinions vary, but it is now generally believed that it is descended from the African, Kaffirian wildcat (*Felis lybica*), rather than from the European wildcat (*Felix sylvestris*). Domestic cats can still breed with either species and share similarities with both.

The Ancient Egyptians were the first people to domesticate cats. They are thought to have started taming local wildcats about 4,000 years ago because they needed them to protect their stored grain from rats and mice. They became great cat lovers, worshipping cats as gods and going into mourning when they died. The remains of many of their pets have been found buried with the Pharaohs in the pyramids. These cats were the probable ancestors of our own domestic cats which are thought to have been brought to Europe in the baggage trains of the Roman legions.

Ancient Egyptian cats probably looked rather like modern Abyssinians which have short brownish hair in which each individual hair is striped. Over the years, such cats developed into the various breeds that we know today which have come to have coats of many different colours. Many are variations on the wild tabby but others are self-coloured black or white or tortiseshell. Some have long hair, like the Persians, while others have none at all, like the bald, sphinx cats.

There are two patterns of tabby fur coats. One rather resembles watered silk and is known as a classic tabby while the other is clearly tiger striped on both sides of the body, and is called a mackerel tabby. Portraits of mackerel tabbies have been found in Egyptian tombs, on Roman mosaics and in many European paintings. Classic tabbies are a later development and were not well established in Europe until the mid-eighteenth century. British short-haired tabbies of both types are recognized in three different colour varieties: silver, red and brown.

RIGHT: The needlework cat opposite is a red, mackerel tabby, commonly known as a marmalade cat. It covers the top of a small round footstool and has been photographed from above.

118

Most domestic moggies are short haired and some of them are striped in shades of orange like the mackerel red tabby or marmalade cat in this design. They are solid, confident cats, intelligent and adaptable and able to fit into almost any domestic environment. They are happy to be fed but are quite capable of catching their own food of small rodents and birds. Natural instincts are never far below the surface and even the best fed cat enjoys stalking and hunting. Cats can be affectionate and many love to be stroked and petted but nevertheless one cannot escape the feeling that life is lived on the cat's terms rather than the owners; sometimes it is difficult to say who has domesticated whom.

The marmalade cat in this design is curled up dozing on a footstool while at the same time staying aware of what is going on by opening its eyes a crack every now and then. A cat seems to spend more time sleeping than any other pet. Indeed, the average adult spends 50 percent of its day in shallow sleep and 15 percent in deep sleep,

leaving only 35 percent of its time awake.

Because cats are neat and precise animals even their sleeping positions are tidy. They will sprawl, stretched out, when basking in the sun but when indoors they often curl up into an almost complete circle with their noses resting on their front paws, their back legs tucked in and their tails almost touching their noses. Many round footstools are cat sized, being about 12 ins (30 cms) in diameter. This suggested the idea of trying to paint a curled-up cat pattern, which when stitched, could be used to cover such a footstool. At a glance the stool covered with this design looks as if a cat is curled up contentedly asleep on top.

WOOL COLOURS AND QUANTITIES

The quantities listed below are the numbers of yards of Elizabeth Bradley wool needed to stitch a piece measuring 124 stitches in diameter on 10 mesh interlock canvas using cross stitch.

Colours used:
14 including 4 background colours

Number on chart key	Elizabeth Bradley wool colours	Quantity (yards)
1	B2	2
2	C1	4
3	C2	9
4	C3	9
5	C5	37
6	C6	48
7	C7	47
8	F3	2
9	G10	2
10	H2	3
11	K10	54
12	L5	32
13	N6	8
14	N4	4

Key numbers 11 and 12 are the background colours and key numbers 13 and 14 are the background crosses.

ABOVE: Another round footstool with a marmalade cat sleeping on top of it. This one has deeper sides which have been covered with a band of the Ivy Border worked on a blue/green (K10) background.

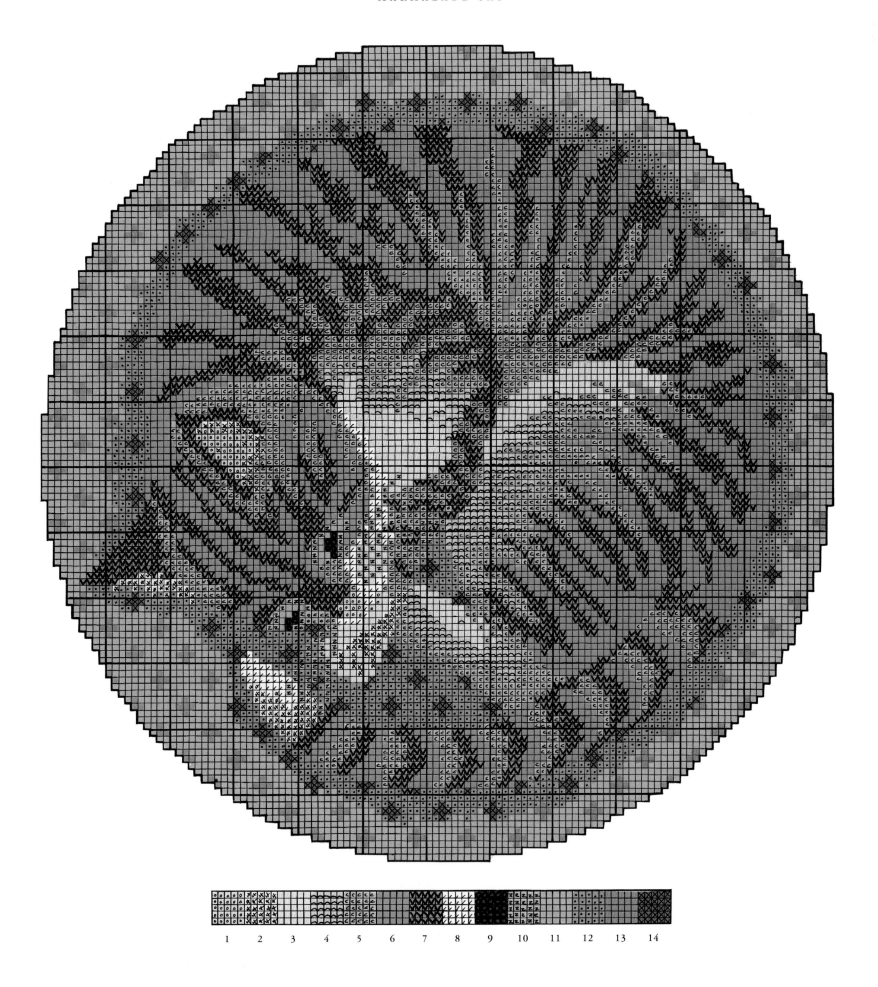

1	2	3	4	5	6	7	8	9	10	11	12	13	14

Chickens

The Galliformes are a large order of birds which are distributed world wide. Mainly seed eating and mostly ground living, they are all chicken-like species which share many similarities. They have plump, rounded and rather squat bodies with short powerful wings which they use for flying in brief explosive bursts. Although they nest and live on the ground they will often fly to escape from predators or up into trees to roost at night. They use their stout, unfeathered legs and strong toenails for scratching and digging for food. They will eat insects and other invertebrates, fruit and berries as well as seeds. The head has a lightly curved beak and often sprouts a crest or wattle. They have abundant feathers and their plumage is usually brightly coloured, especially the male's. There are seven families in the order and the ancestor of our domestic chickens, the jungle fowl (*Gallus gallus*), belongs to the Phasianidae, or pheasants.

The red jungle fowl, which lives wild over a large part of Asia, looks very similar to the old sporting breed of chicken called old English game; such birds were kept for fighting rather than for the pot. Poultry keeping was practised by the early Egyptians and apparently flourished in Britain even before the Romans arrived. Caesar tells us that the Britons "kept fowls for pleasure and diversion" though for some unknown reason it was unlawful to eat them. From medieval times until well into the nineteenth century, cock fighting was practically a national sport with a well-documented history of lore, practice and prime blood lines.

WOOL COLOURS AND QUANTITIES

The quantities listed below are the numbers of yards of Elizabeth Bradley wool needed to stitch a piece measuring 277 stitches by 205 stitches on 10 mesh interlock canvas using cross stitch.

Colours used: 27

Number on chart key	Elizabeth Bradley wool colours	Quantity (yards)
1	B10	12
2	C1	50
3	C3	370
4	C5	9
5	C6	9
6	C7	19
7	C11	25
8	D2	9
9	D3	9
10	D4	6
11	E2	84
12	E5	92
13	E8	84
14	E9	76
15	E11	21
16	F8	13
17	F9	13
18	G10	16
19	I1	22
20	I4	23
21	J5	42
22	J6	43
23	J9	55
24	K9	10
25	K10	23
26	K11	30
27	L7	15

RIGHT: The chickens and their chicks are standing on a typical Victorian island of grass with a few flowers and a patch of bare earth or sand in the foreground. Behind them is a small lake and some trees. The scene has been worked against a soft golden yellow (C3) background and edged with a needlework frame. It measures 27.7ins (70.5cms) by 20.6ins (52.5cms) and so will fit easily across a piece of interlock canvas 39ins (1m) wide.

Chickens make good subjects for selective breeding and over the years all sorts of specialized breeds have been developed, divided loosely into laying breeds, table breeds, general purpose breeds and exhibition breeds and bantams. A modern addition to this list should be breeds suitable for battery cages, broiler houses and intensive chicken farming. This sort of breeding is controlled by large companies rather than by farmers or fanciers, as it was in the past. Recently there has been a resurgence of interest in old breeds as concern for the welfare of battery chickens has grown. The public are increasingly demanding free range chickens and eggs rather than those from battery houses.

The group of chickens on this design is taken from a Victorian Berlin woolwork panel that I acquired during my years as an antique textile dealer. It dates from about 1860 which was a prime time for fancy poultry breeding, the first poultry show having been held at the London zoo in 1845. The cock and the hen on the right are both gold pencilled Hamburghs. Bred mainly as exhibition fowl they are small birds with slender, dark, clean legs and rose combs. The colour of the cock's breast and saddle is known as red bay and its hackle or neck feathers are bronze. The pencilled feathers of the hen are gold laced with black. This breed is not good at incubating its own eggs and so the chicks would probably be hatched by a hen of another breed such as an old English game or a Sussex.

The hen on the left is paler in colour and mottled rather than marbled in cream and brown. She looks like a cross between a silver pencilled Hamburgh and a silkie, a small white bantam with a puff of feathers like an elegant hat on its head and rather ridiculous feathered feet.

OVERLEAF: Collage: old-fashioned, fancy breeds of chickens living free range on an upland farm.

1 2 3 4 5 6 7 8 9 10 11 12 13 14 15 16 17 18 19 20 21 22 23 24 25 26 27

Pointer

How dogs first became domesticated is unknown as it happened way back in prehistoric times. Possibly, orphan wolf cubs were taken back to camp and brought up with caveman children and the relationship carried on from there. Dogs (*Canis familiaris*) share many instincts with their wolf ancestors including a strong sense of territory and a natural ability and desire to hunt, they also have the same sharp ears and exceptional sense of smell.

Prehistoric man gradually changed from being a hunter to a gatherer and grower of

ABOVE: This Pointer needlework is enhanced by an old rosewood frame.

food and dogs developed along with him. Some were still bred for the chase while others were encouraged to be shepherd dogs for collecting and guarding the herds and flocks of newly domesticated animals. Hunting dogs were trained to use their natural skills to assist their masters with various aspects of hunting. They helped to track down the prey and flush it out from where it was hiding, then helped to kill it and, if it had been killed with an arrow or spear some distance away, retrieve it.

WOOL COLOURS AND QUANTITIES

The quantities listed below are the numbers of yards of Elizabeth Bradley wool needed to work a piece measuring 150 stitches by 100 stitches on 10 mesh interlock canvas using cross stitch.

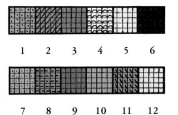

1 2 3 4 5 6

7 8 9 10 11 12

Colours used: 12 colours

Number on chart key	Elizabeth Bradley wool colour	Quantity (yards)
1	E2	16
2	E5	14
3	E7	74
4	F3	7
5	F5	80
6	G10	2
7	J4	8
8	J6	23
9	J8	23
10	J10	16
11	K5	7
12	L2	56

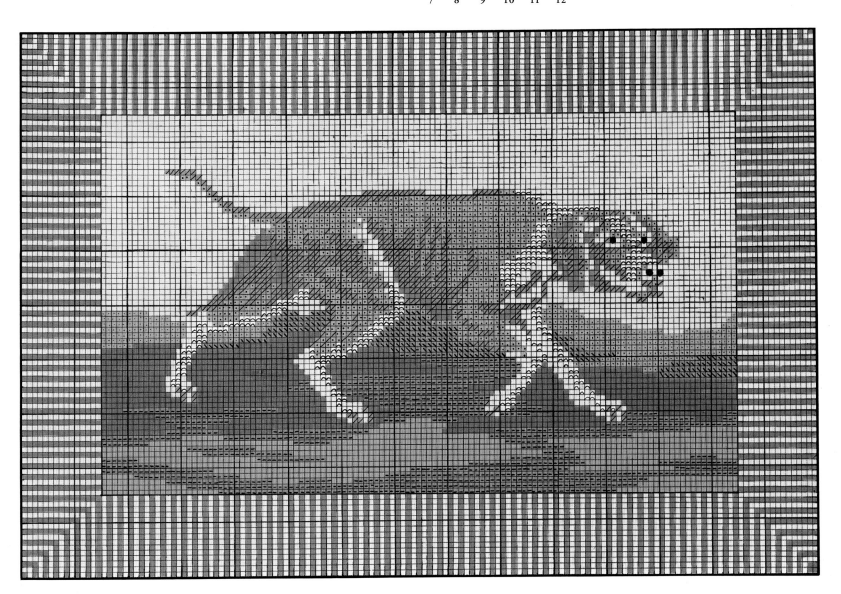

Different breeds of dogs gradually developed around the world, each suitable for its own particular job, environment and conditions. Out on grassy plains or in open desert, sight and speed are more useful than hearing and smell and so over the centuries long legged, fast running dogs evolved. These were the early ancestors of the swift and elegant hunting hounds such as whippets, greyhounds, salukis and borzois. On the other hand, European gundogs often work in woodland and undergrowth so they have to be able to smell their prey rather than see it. Acute scenting ability is found in dogs with long noses and ears, pendulous hanging lips and large, open nostrils – all features which are pronounced in modern pointers, setters and spaniels.

The Pointer design

The dog in this needlework design is a pointer. They are an interesting breed of dogs displaying an accentuated facet of what must have been normal hunting behaviour. Unlike hounds, pointers track by air scent and aid hunters to find and retrieve birds and other small game. These dogs range well ahead of their owners, often out of sight. When they scent game they stand frozen a few yards (metres) away from the hidden prey, pointing towards it. They should remain in this position until the hunter flushes out and kills it. A well-trained pointer will hold a point for up to two hours, quietly waiting until the game is shot and the command to find and retrieve are given.

This needlework dog is on point, tense and expectant against a background of rough grass and blue sky. The central part of the pattern is taken from an old chart, the original dating from about 1840, and the look of the dog in it is very characteristic of this period. Pointers first appeared in Britain in around 1650 when they were used to point hares for coursing greyhounds. When shooting birds with shot pellets became popular early in the eighteenth century, they changed their attention almost exclusively to game birds. The breed came originally from Spain and the name is derived from the Spanish word *punta* or point. This needlework dog is a heavier animal than a typical Spanish pointer and so is probably English; originally developed by breeding Spanish dogs with foxhounds and greyhounds to give them more speed.

Borders and frames

He is framed by a simple but effective border of parallel lines worked in brown and beige. This adds elegance to the small central design so making it easier to use. Finished pointer pieces make rather smart oblong cushions, they also look handsome framed like the one on the previous page. The rose wood frame that I used is an old one from about the same time as the original chart was painted.

RIGHT: Collage: pointers out early on a frosty morning.

Pig Pillow

This pink porker is a middle white and is a fine example of one of the rarest breeds of British pigs. Popular in the first half of the twentieth century, few animals now exist in Britain though there are flourishing herds of middle whites in the Far East and Japan. In fact, they are held in such high regard in Japan that a memorial has recently been erected to three exceptional boars of the breed.

Modern pig breeds (*Sus scrosa*) are derived from a mixture of European and Asiatic wild ancestors. Until the middle of the eighteenth century there were two types of native swine in Europe, small dark ones with prick ears and large pink or dark coloured pigs with lop ears. They lived almost wild, in the care of swineherds, foraging about for food in the woods, on the hillsides and along the seashore. Smaller and fatter varieties, that were used to being kept confined, were brought back to Europe from Asia half way through the century and interbred with the larger native pigs. The resulting breeds did well in the more restricted conditions caused by the enclosure of common land and thrived on small holdings and farms until they in their turn were made obsolete by the advent of factory farming. Middle whites are a speciality pork pig derived from a cross between large whites and the now extinct small white in the mid-nineteenth century. They are middle sized, all-pink pigs with dished faces and rather endearing squashed and wrinkled snouts.

In the last forty years the breeding emphasis has changed to bacon pigs which are suit-able for intensive rearing in indoor pig units. The recent reaction against such farming methods has revived interest in the older breeds which are better suited to life outdoors in a more natural environment. Such pigs can often survive on lower energy feed than modern types and now that much farmland in Europe is unused could once again be useful residents for empty fields. Older breeds of livestock are interesting not only as curiosities but also because they are part of our social history. It has also been realized that the loss of old breeds of domestic animals might be regretted for scientific reasons; once they become extinct their genetic material is gone for ever.

ABOVE: This needlework pig can be worked without the border and looks effective against many different background colours.

OVERLEAF: Collage: a cheerful group of pigs in a barn full of clean straw.

132

The Pig Pillow design

This woolwork middle white pig stands on a grassy island framed by a border of country flowers such as might surround a pig if it was lucky enough to live in a field. I am fond of pigs and had a pet pig called Abigail many years ago, so it seems quite reasonable to me to put one in the centre of such a pretty border though I can understand that it might seem rather inappropriate to many people. The finished model shown here is just the right size for a pillow-sized cushion. It has been worked on a pale pink (B1) background because I think it added to the rosy charm of the design. But, if pink is not a favourite colour for you, then cream (F3) or pale blue (L1) would be equally pretty. Black (G11) or dark blue (L11) would work well as darker alternatives.

ABOVE: I developed a passion for pink backgrounds when I was writing this book. The background colour used on the Pig Pillow shown here is pink (B1) and is one of my favourites.

WOOL COLOURS AND QUANTITIES

The quantities listed below are the numbers of yards of Elizabeth Bradley wool needed to stitch a piece measuring 162 stitches by 241 stitches on 10 mesh interlock canvas using cross stitch.

Colours used:
31 including 1 background colour

Number on chart key	Elizabeth Bradley wool colours	Quantity (yards)
1	A6	14
2	A9	21
3	A10	17
4	B1	294
5	B2	32
6	B3	50
7	B4	55
8	B5	16
9	B10	37
10	B11	14
11	C5	18
12	C6	13
13	D4	12
14	D8	7
15	D9	9
16	D11	6
17	E8	6
18	G10	17
19	J3	18
20	J4	33
21	J5	33
22	J8	45
23	J10	36
24	J11	31
25	K6	17
26	L8	17
27	L9	12
28	L10	13
29	M3	11
30	N7	5
31	N11	5

Key number 4
is the background colour.

1 2 3 4 5 6 7 8 9 10 11 12 13 14 15 16

17 18 19 20 21 22 23 24 25 26 27 28 29 30 31

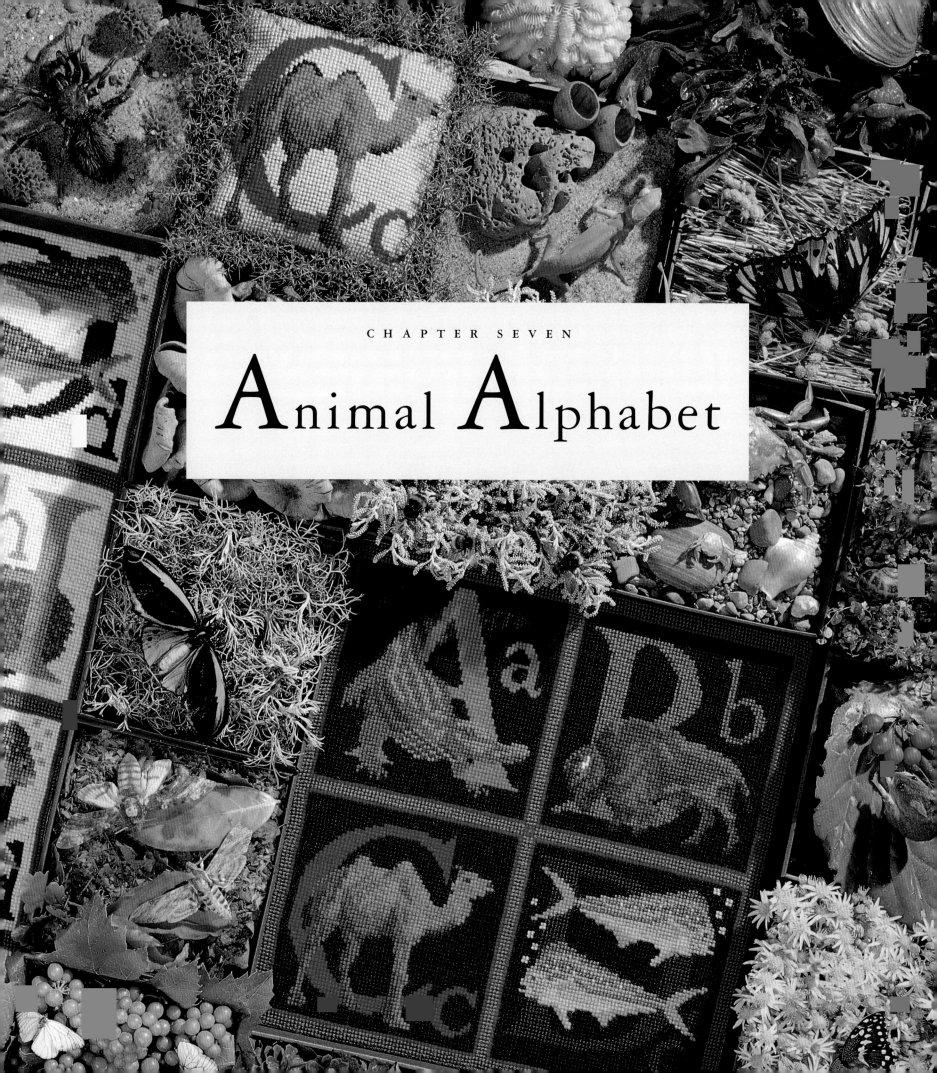

Animal Alphabet

Animal Alphabet

Stitching an embroidered alphabet has been a standard part of many children's education for the last 400 years; in fact, it is only relatively recently that the practice has been abandoned. Both I in the 1950s and my daughter Anna in the 1970s, worked simple alphabets at school.

Before books were widely available, children often learned their alphabet by stitching neat rows of letters from various styles of alphabet onto pieces of linen called samplers or exemplars. The capital letters from such alphabets could then be used to mark household and personal linen, the initials of the owner being stitched in minute cross stitches in red or black thread. This practice was necessary in the days when washing and ironing was often done by specialist washerwomen who made their living by collecting laundry from a number of houses and then returning it freshly washed and starched. Before the days of name tapes, everything from school uniform to sheets and shirts had to be identified by embroidered initials.

Some alphabets were plain and some were elaborate. Succeeding generations of children copied letters from their mothers' and grandmothers' samplers. In addition, books and sheets showing all sorts of alphabet patterns were readily available from the mid-eighteenth century onwards. The Victorians, with their passion for cross stitch in both wool and silk, went one step further by producing all sorts of fancy and pictorial alphabets. Charts showing letters entwined with flowers or adorned with curlicues, Gothic arches or baroque scrolls, were often published in ladies' magazines or could be bought from specialist needlework emporia.

In recent years, working cross-stitch designs on linen has regained popularity as a pastime. Enthusiasts embroider all manner of objects from elaborate pictures and samplers to tiny Christmas cards and bookmarks. Many different alphabet designs are now being produced. Some of them feature flowers, fruit or animals, while others are based on illustrations from children's books such as Kate Greenaway or characters from cartoons, nursery rhymes and fairy stories.

This animal alphabet was great fun to paint. I made the animals relatively simple in style because it seemed appropriate and it made them more suitable for use in children's rooms. I also thought that children might like to try to work some of the letters as many of them are quite easy and straightforward to stitch. I made the squares as bright as our range of wool and the actual colours of the animals allowed. Each letter is a different colour, though this can be changed to suit individual projects or to add variety to words featuring several of the same letter. Sometimes it is also advisable to change the colours so they show up better against a particular background colour. For example, on the pale green HAPPY BIRTHDAY rug on page 152, the two Hs were worked in bright yellow (D7) instead of the pale limey green (I1) shown on the chart. The yellow was much more effective than the green which tended to merge with the background colour.

WOOL COLOURS AND QUANTITIES

The wool quantities listed by each chart on pages 141-155 are the numbers of yards of Elizabeth Bradley wool needed to work the individual letters, numbers and spacers of the Animal Alphabet. Each small square measures 62 stitches by 62 stitches and is worked on 10 mesh interlock canvas using cross stitch.

The background colours of the various worked pieces shown in this chapter are given below. If black (G11) is to be used for the background colour, then G10 should be substituted by G9 wherever it occurs.

The background colours of the worked pieces shown in this chapter are as follows:

The ABCD picture shown on page 138, black (G11).

The bolster shown on page 143, cream (F3).

The C for Camel cushion shown on page 147, pale blue (L1).

The play cube shown on page 147, pale blue (L1).

The Animal Alphabet carpet shown on page 148, cream (F3).

The 10 YRS OLD cushion shown on page 149, pale pink (B1).

The HAPPY BIRTHDAY rug shown on page 152, pale green (J2).

The 1-9 cushion shown on page 155, pale blue (L1).

PREVIOUS PAGE: Needlework Animal Alphabet squares are mixed with square boxes filled with a variety of natural materials and small animals.

LETTER A
Alligator

Colours used:

6 plus one background colour

Number on chart key	Elizabeth Bradley wool colour	Quantity (yards)
1	B11	5
2	C10	12
3	D11	5
4	F11	5
5	I4	8
6	I9	10

Background quantity for a piece measuring 62 stitches by 62 stitches: 48 yards.

LETTER B
Buffalo

Colours used:

10 plus one background colour

Number on chart key	Elizabeth Bradley wool colour	Quantity (yards)
1	B11	5
2	F3	1
3	G5	5
4	G6	7
5	G7	4
6	G10	1
7	H3	4
8	H4	5
9	H5	4
10	J6	16

Background quantity for a piece measuring 62 stitches by 62 stitches: 50 yards.

LETTER C
Camel

Colours used:

6 plus one background colour

Number on chart key	Elizabeth Bradley wool colour	Quantity (yards)
1	B11	18
2	E4	7
3	E5	7
4	F9	9
5	F11	5
6	G10	2

Background quantity for a piece measuring 62 stitches by 62 stitches: 40 yards.

LETTER D
Dorado

Colours used:

9 plus one background colour

Number on chart key	Elizabeth Bradley wool colour	Quantity (yards)
1	B11	5
2	C5	4
3	D4	5
4	I1	3
5	J10	8
6	J6	3
7	L1	3
8	L10	6
9	L11	13

Background quantity for a piece measuring 62 stitches by 62 stitches: 33 yards.

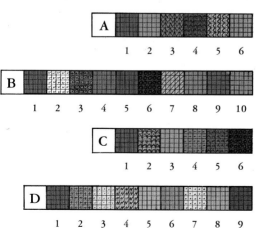

A   1 2 3 4 5 6

B   1 2 3 4 5 6 7 8 9 10

C   1 2 3 4 5 6

D   1 2 3 4 5 6 7 8 9

LETTER E
Elephant

Colours used:

8 plus one background colour

Number on chart key	Elizabeth Bradley wool colour	Quantity (yards)
1	B11	5
2	A3	10
3	C1	1
4	G10	1
5	H8	10
6	H9	9
7	H10	8
8	H11	4

Background quantity for a
piece measuring 62 stitches by
62 stitches: 18 yards.

LETTER F
Falcon

Colours used:

11 plus one background colour

Number on chart key	Elizabeth Bradley wool colour	Quantity (yards)
1	B11	5
2	C1	3
3	D7	14
4	E1	4
5	E2	2
6	E9	3
7	G10	3
8	J6	5
9	H9	3
10	H10	3
11	H11	4

Background quantity for a
piece measuring 62 stitches by
62 stitches: 42 yards.

LETTER H
Hedgehog

Colours used:

8 plus one background colour

Number on chart key	Elizabeth Bradley wool colour	Quantity (yards)
1	B11	5
2	E2	4
3	F7	6
4	F10	4
5	G8	1
6	G10	1
7	G5	7
8	I1	25

Background quantity for a
piece measuring 62 stitches by
62 stitches: 40 yards.

LETTER G
Giraffe

Colours used:

8 plus one background colour

Number on chart key	Elizabeth Bradley wool colour	Quantity (yards)
1	B11	5
2	C1	9
3	E1	4
4	E8	5
5	E9	6
6	E11	3
7	G10	2
8	N9	13

Background quantity for a
piece measuring 62 stitches by
62 stitches: 33 yards.

The animals in the alphabet

You will probably wonder why some of the animals featured in this alphabet are so obscure. Why, for instance, D for dorado and not D for dog or donkey, and why Q for quetzal, and what on earth is a quetzal anyway? The quetzal is, in fact, one of only two animals beginning with the letter Q. Although you may never of heard of it, it is actually one of the most beautiful birds in the world. It lives in South America and was regarded as sacred by the Mayans and Aztecs and is now the national bird of Guatemala. U for uja and X for xenosaurus were chosen for very similar reasons, they were really the only candidates available for their letter of the alphabet.

The other factor that influenced my choice of animals was that this book is destined to be translated into French and Italian and so the alphabet had to work in all three languages. This, not surprisingly, caused some difficulties. For instance, the only animals that start with D in all three languages are dorado and dromedary, and I could not use D for dromedary as I had already used C for camel. So it had to be D for dorado!

A dorado, or dolphin fish, is a large, brightly coloured fish that is common in warm seas. It is usually caught on a line and it tastes delicious, especially when barbecued. Sadly, when caught, it loses all its beautiful colours almost immediately and so the dorados you see for sale in markets or fish shops are all grey.

The Alphabet

	English	*French*	*Italian*
A is for	Alligator	Alligator	Alligatore
B is for	Buffalo	Buffle	Bufalo
C is for	Camel	Chameau	Cammello
D is for	Dorado	Dorade	Delfino
E is for	Elephant	Elephant	Elefante
F is for	Falcon	Faucon	Falco
G is for	Giraffe	Girafe	Giraffa
H is for	Hedgehog	Herisson	
I is for	Iguana	Iguane	Iguana
J is for	Jaguar	Jaguar	
K is for	Koala	Koala	Koala
L is for	Lion	Lion	Leone
M is for	Mallard	Mulard	Mallardo
N is for	Narwhal	Narval	Narvalo
O is for	Orang-utan	Orang-utan	Orango
P is for	Parrot	Perroquet	Pappagallo
Q is for	Quetzal	Quetzal	Quetzal
R is for	Reindeer	Renne	Renna
S is for	Salmon	Saumon	Salmone
T is for	Terrapin	Tortue	Tartaruga
U is for	Uja	Uja	Uja
V is for	Viper	Vipere	Vipera
W is for	Wallaby	Wallaby	Wallaby
X is for	Xenosaurus	Xenosaurus	Xenosaurus
Y is for	Yak	Yak	Yak
Z is for	Zebra	Zebre	Zebra

There are no animals beginning with the letters H or J in Italian.

ABOVE: *A bolster made from four rows of four squares worked on a cream (F3) background.*

143

LETTER I
Iguana

Colours used:
8 plus one background colour

Number on chart key	Elizabeth Bradley wool colour	Quantity (yards)
1	B11	5
2	F9	10
3	G10	9
4	I1	9
5	I4	4
6	J6	3
7	J10	8
8	N11	9

Background quantity for a piece measuring 62 stitches by 62 stitches: 33 yards.

LETTER J
Jaguar

Colours used:
8 plus one background colour

Number on chart key	Elizabeth Bradley wool colour	Quantity (yards)
1	B11	5
2	C1	5
3	C2	5
4	C3	4
5	C5	5
6	C8	2
7	G10	8
8	L5	10

Background quantity for a piece measuring 62 stitches by 62 stitches: 37 yards.

LETTER K
Koala

Colours used:
7 plus one background colour

Number on chart key	Elizabeth Bradley wool colour	Quantity (yards)
1	B11	5
2	C8	13
3	G10	1
4	H6	1
5	H8	11
6	H9	8
7	H10	8

Background quantity for a piece measuring 62 stitches by 62 stitches: 33 yards.

LETTER L
Lion

Colours used:
10 plus one background colour

Number on chart key	Elizabeth Bradley wool colour	Quantity (yards)
1	B11	5
2	A3	1
3	C1	1
4	E4	4
5	E5	12
6	F9	6
7	F11	9
8	G9	4
9	G10	1
10	J10	10

Background quantity for a piece measuring 62 stitches by 62 stitches: 37 yards.

LETTER M
Mallard

Colours used:

12 plus one background colour

Number on chart key	Elizabeth Bradley wool colour	Quantity (yards)
1	B11	5
2	C2	1
3	C8	1
4	F1	2
5	F5	7
6	F6	3
7	F9	4
8	G10	5
9	H2	3
10	H3	3
11	K11	3
12	N5	23

Background quantity for a piece measuring 62 stitches by 62 stitches: 38 yards.

LETTER N
Narwhal

Colours used:

8 plus one background colour

Number on chart key	Elizabeth Bradley wool colour	Quantity (yards)
1	B11	5
2	A5	18
3	F5	3
4	F6	3
5	F7	5
6	H3	3
7	H5	2
8	L10	1

Background quantity for a piece measuring 62 stitches by 62 stitches: 41 yards.

LETTER O
Orang utan

Colours used:

8 plus one background colour

Number on chart key	Elizabeth Bradley wool colour	Quantity (yards)
1	B11	5
2	C11	10
3	E8	6
4	E9	4
5	G10	1
6	H3	2
7	H5	4
8	L10	18

Background quantity for a piece measuring 62 stitches by 62 stitches: 35 yards.

LETTER P
Parrot

Colours used:

8 plus one background colour

Number on chart key	Elizabeth Bradley wool colour	Quantity (yards)
1	B11	8
2	C5	18
3	H5	3
4	H10	3
5	I1	5
6	J6	8
7	J8	3
8	L5	3

Background quantity for a piece measuring 62 stitches by 62 stitches: 38 yards.

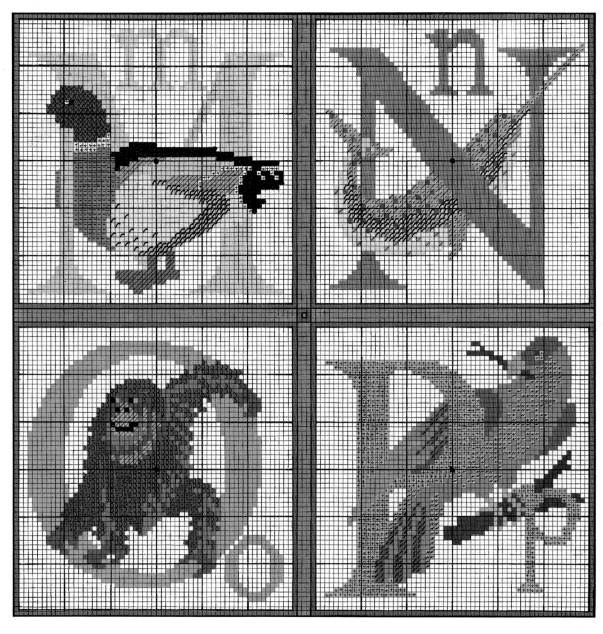

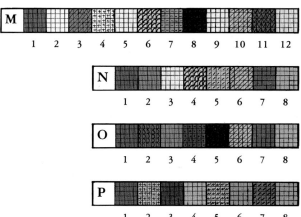

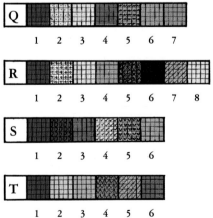

LETTER Q
Quetzal

Colours used:

7 plus one background colour

Number on chart key	Elizabeth Bradley wool colour	Quantity (yards)
1	B11	7
2	D4	13
3	F5	3
4	H5	4
5	I1	8
6	J10	4
7	K10	11

Background quantity for a piece measuring 62 stitches by 62 stitches: 35 yards.

LETTER R
Reindeer

Colours used:

8 plus one background colour

Number on chart key	Elizabeth Bradley wool colour	Quantity (yards)
1	B11	5
2	F1	5
3	F5	5
4	G4	7
5	G5	8
6	G10	1
7	H3	3
8	M6	17

Background quantity for a piece measuring 62 stitches by 62 stitches: 38 yards.

LETTER S
Salmon

Colours used:

6 plus one background colour

Number on chart key	Elizabeth Bradley wool colour	Quantity (yards)
1	B11	5
2	C11	13
3	H5	10
4	H8	5
5	H9	7
6	H10	5

Background quantity for a piece measuring 62 stitches by 62 stitches: 40 yards.

LETTER T
Terrapin

Colours used:

6 plus one background colour

Number on chart key	Elizabeth Bradley wool colour	Quantity (yards)
1	B11	5
2	C9	14
3	D9	10
4	D11	8
5	H3	1
6	H5	8

Background quantity for a piece measuring 62 stitches by 62 stitches: 38 yards.

*Some suggested uses for
Alphabet and Number Squares*

- A play cube to be used as a soft toy
- A carpet featuring the complete alphabet
- A square cushion featuring numbers 1 to 9
- A small carpet that spells a message or name, eg HAPPY BIRTHDAY
- A cushion to give as a present or to celebrate a special occasion. For example, LOVE or WELCOME or MARY SEPT 1970
- A single row of squares to hang across the top of a nursery or playroom window to act as a pelmet
- A long line of squares to act as a frieze to go around the top of nursery, playroom or bedroom walls
- A row of single squares to be hung vertically in a room like a long bell pull. They could spell a name or a message such as CONGRATULATIONS, ADAM'S ROOM or the full name of a child.

*RIGHT: A play cube and a small cushion
made from Animal Alphabet squares.
Both pieces were worked on pale blue (L1)
backgrounds. The chair is a nineteenth-
century child's chair.*

LEFT: A carpet or wall hanging featuring the complete Animal Alphabet. The background colour is cream (F3). The carpet is edged with six rows of grass green (J6) with the two outermost, edging rows being red (B11). The squares at either end of the bottom row of the carpet are ladybird spacers.

WOOL COLOURS AND QUANTITIES -

a complete alphabet carpet

The quantities listed below are the numbers of yards of Elizabeth Bradley wool needed to work the carpet shown opposite. The piece measures 273 stitches by 468 stitches and is worked on 10 mesh interlock canvas using cross stitch.

Colours used:
69 plus one background colour

Elizabeth Bradley wool colours	Quantity (yards)
A3	12
A5	18
B10	28
B11	220
C1	17
C2	7
C3	4
C4	12
C5	28
C8	16
C9	13
C10	10
C11	23
D4	18
D7	13
D9	9
D11	12
E1	19
E2	13
E4	12
E5	24
E8	10
E9	12
E10	8
E11	3
F1	16
F3	1
F5	19
F6	15
F7	10
F8	15
F9	28
F10	16
F11	18
G4	6
G5	18
G6	6
G7	3
G8	12
G9	3
G10	75

Elizabeth Bradley wool colours	Quantity (yards)
H2	2
H3	26
H4	5
H5	43
H6	8
H8	26
H9	26
H10	26
H11	8
I1	43
I4	12
I9	9
J6	225
J8	15
J9	2
J10	25
K10	20
K11	2
L1	2
L5	12
L10	25
L11	13
M2	15
M6	18
N5	23
N9	12
N10	16
N11	8

Background quantity for the carpet:
1,026 yards.

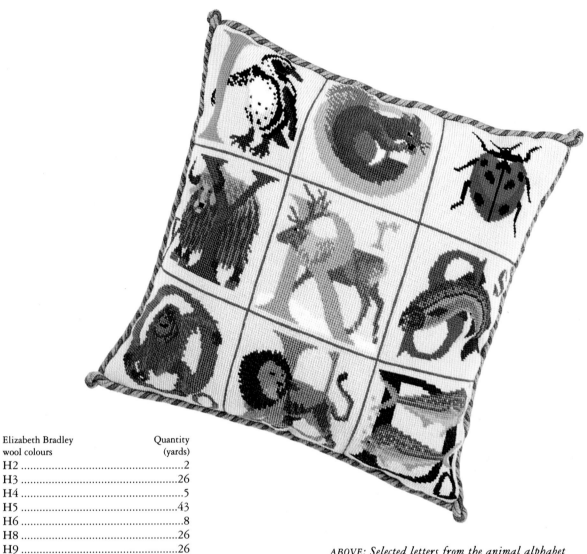

ABOVE: Selected letters from the animal alphabet have been combined on this cushion to spell out 10 yrs old. The ladybird spacer has been used to fill in the remaining square.

The Ladybird and Spider Spacers

These two squares (see page 151) do not feature a letter or a number but just an animal on its own, one shows a ladybird and the other a garden spider. The squares have been designed to be used as fillers or spacers and the alphabet carpet opposite illustrates their use. On this piece, rather than leaving two blank squares at the end of the 26 letters of the alphabet, two ladybird squares have been used to fill up the extra space.

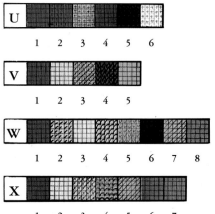

U 1 2 3 4 5 6

V 1 2 3 4 5

W 1 2 3 4 5 6 7 8

X 1 2 3 4 5 6 7

LETTER U
Uja

Colours used:

6 plus one background colour

Number on chart key	Elizabeth Bradley wool colour	Quantity (yards)
1	B11	5
2	B10	18
3	C5	1
4	G8	11
5	G10	13
6	F1	3

Background quantity for a piece measuring 62 stitches by 62 stitches: 38 yards.

LETTER V
Viper

Colours used:

5 plus one background colour

Number on chart key	Elizabeth Bradley wool colour	Quantity (yards)
1	B11	5
2	E1	8
3	E2	5
4	E10	9
5	K10	11

Background quantity for a piece measuring 62 stitches by 62 stitches: 42 yards.

LETTER W
Wallaby

Colours used:

8 plus one background colour

Number on chart key	Elizabeth Bradley wool colour	Quantity (yards)
1	B11	5
2	C4	12
3	F5	2
4	F6	9
5	F8	4
6	G10	1
7	H3	1
8	H5	2

Background quantity for a piece measuring 62 stitches by 62 stitches: 42 yards.

LETTER X
Xenosaurus

Colours used:

7 plus one background colour

Number on chart key	Elizabeth Bradley wool colour	Quantity (yards)
1	B11	5
2	E1	4
3	E2	3
4	E4	2
5	H3	6
6	H5	5
7	N10	17

Background quantity for a piece measuring 62 stitches by 62 stitches: 42 yards.

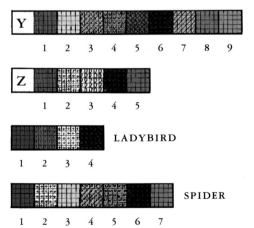

Y									
1	2	3	4	5	6	7	8	9	

Z				
1	2	3	4	5

LADYBIRD

1	2	3	4

SPIDER

1	2	3	4	5	6	7

LETTER Y
Yak

Colours used:

9 plus one background colour

Number on chart key	Elizabeth Bradley wool colour	Quantity (yards)
1	B11	5
2	E1	1
3	E2	6
4	F8	11
5	F10	12
6	G10	1
7	H3	3
8	H5	5
9	M2	15

Background quantity for a
piece measuring 62 stitches by
62 stitches: 33 yards.

LETTER Z
Zebra

Colours used:

5 plus one background colour

Number on chart key	Elizabeth Bradley wool colour	Quantity (yards)
1	B11	5
2	F1	3
3	H6	7
4	G10	14
5	J9	15

Background quantity for a
piece measuring 62 stitches by
62 stitches: 38 yards.

LADYBIRD SPACER

Colours used:

4 plus one background colour

Number on chart key	Elizabeth Bradley wool colour	Quantity (yards)
1	B11	11
2	B10	6
3	F1	1
4	G10	11

Background quantity for a
piece measuring 62 stitches by
62 stitches: 58 yards.

SPIDER SPACER

Colours used:

7 plus one background colour

Number on chart key	Elizabeth Bradley wool colour	Quantity (yards)
1	B11	5
2	F1	2
3	E1	7
4	E2	3
5	F8	5
6	G10	3
7	H5	6

Background quantity for a
piece measuring 62 stitches by
62 stitches: 50 yards.

ABOVE: *This Happy Birthday rug or wall hanging has been worked on a pale green (J2) background. The two letters 'H' have been worked in bright yellow (D7) rather than pale lime green (I1) because yellow showed up better against the green background. The squares at either end of the bottom row are spider spacers.*

Numbers

These ten number squares (see charts on pages 153-5) were designed to complement the alphabet. They can be used on their own or in combination with the alphabet squares. The numbers 1-9 worked as a piece can be made into a cushion which is both decorative and educational for small children. The numbers are also useful when composing birthday or anniversary messages such as MARY BORN 2 3 95 or 25 YRS or 12 YRS OLD.

Descriptions of the number squares

0 SQUIRREL IN A RING

1 PENGUIN

2 ANGEL FISH

3 DORMICE

4 BEETLES

5 LEGS OF A STARFISH

6 HOLLY BLUE BUTTERFLIES

7 GOLDFISH

8 TENTACLES OF AN OCTOPUS

9 BUMBLE BEES

NUMBER 1

Colours used:

6 plus one background colour

Number on chart key	Elizabeth Bradley wool colour	Quantity (yards)
1	B11	5
2	A3	12
3	F1	7
4	H6	6
5	G10	12
6	H5	7

Background quantity for a piece measuring 62 stitches by 62 stitches: 50 yards.

NUMBER 2

Colours used:

7 plus one background colour

Number on chart key	Elizabeth Bradley wool colour	Quantity (yards)
1	B11	5
2	A5	5
3	G10	5
4	I1	14
5	J6	6
6	L5	6
7	N5	15

Background quantity for a piece measuring 62 stitches by 62 stitches: 38 yards.

NUMBER 3

Colours used:

8 plus one background colour

Number on chart key	Elizabeth Bradley wool colour	Quantity (yards)
1	B11	5
2	B2	2
3	C8	9
4	E1	3
5	E2	6
6	G5	18
7	G10	1
8	H5	3

Background quantity for a piece measuring 62 stitches by 62 stitches: 38 yards.

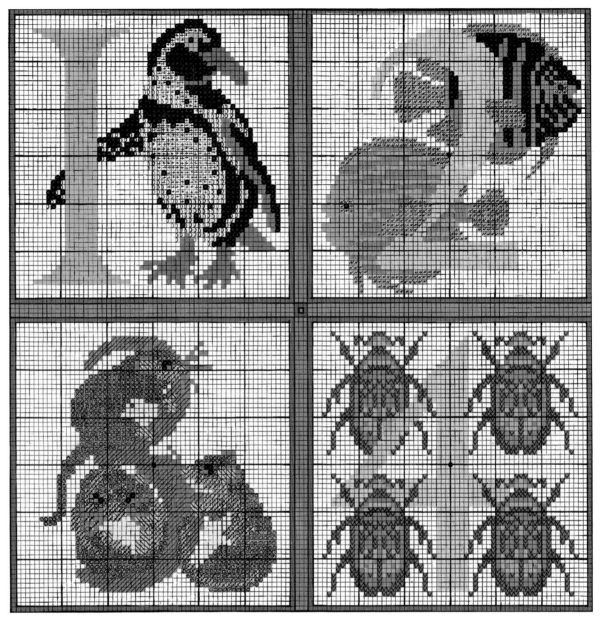

NUMBER 4

Colours used:

5 plus one background colour

Number on chart key	Elizabeth Bradley wool colour	Quantity (yards)
1	B11	11
2	D7	13
3	J6	9
4	K11	18
5	J10	5

Background quantity for a piece measuring 62 stitches by 62 stitches: 38 yards.

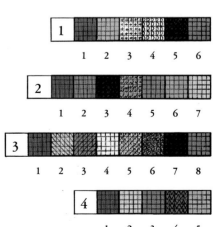

Colours used:

4 plus one background colour

Number on chart key	Elizabeth Bradley wool colour	Quantity (yards)
1	B11	20
2	B10	15
3	F1	7
4	M11	14

Background quantity for a
piece measuring 62 stitches by
62 stitches: 38 yards.

NUMBER 6

Colours used:

5 plus one background colour

Number on chart key	Elizabeth Bradley wool colour	Quantity (yards)
1	B11	5
2	C9	13
3	H5	11
4	H9	1
5	M6	12

Background quantity for a
piece measuring 62 stitches by
62 stitches: 45 yards.

NUMBER 7

Colours used:

8 plus one background colour

Number on chart key	Elizabeth Bradley wool colour	Quantity (yards)
1	B11	5
2	C5	7
3	C6	8
4	C7	10
5	C8	11
6	G10	6
7	H5	3
8	J10	10

Background quantity for a
piece measuring 62 stitches by
62 stitches: 38 yards.

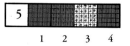

5   1   2   3   4

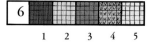

6   1   2   3   4   5

7   1   2   3   4   5   6   7   8

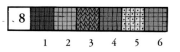

8   1   2   3   4   5   6

NUMBER 8

Colours used:

6 plus one background colour

Number on chart key	Elizabeth Bradley wool colour	Quantity (yards)
1	B11	5
2	D9	15
3	D11	8
4	H5	9
5	L1	5
6	M2	14

Background quantity for a
piece measuring 62 stitches by
62 stitches: 34 yards.

NUMBER 9

Colours used:

5 plus one background colour

Number on chart key	Elizabeth Bradley wool colour	Quantity (yards)
1	B11	5
2	B10	14
3	D7	3
4	E1	9
5	G10	10

Background quantity for a piece measuring 62 stitches by 62 stitches: 40 yards.

NUMBER 0

Colours used:

8 plus one background colour

Number on chart key	Elizabeth Bradley wool colour	Quantity (yards)
1	B11	5
2	B3	20
3	C11	12
4	E8	15
5	E9	9
6	F1	2
7	G10	1
8	H4	4

Background quantity for a piece measuring 62 stitches by 62 stitches: 35 yards.

BELOW: The numbers 1 to 9 fit together very neatly to make a square cushion. This one is worked on a pale blue (L1) background.

9				
1	2	3	4	5

0							
1	2	3	4	5	6	7	8

Materials and Methods

Canvas for woolwork

Woolwork is normally worked on special machine-woven canvas which is available in a variety of colours and sizes. This canvas is described or measured by the number of mesh per inch (a mesh being the intersection where two threads cross). Ten mesh canvas has ten threads and ten holes per inch.

All the woolwork designs in this book have been worked on a type of canvas known as interlock canvas which was developed comparatively recently as a variation on the older and more conventional single threaded, mono canvas or double threaded, Penelope canvas. On these canvases the horizontal (weft) threads pass under and over the vertical (warp) threads as is normal on most woven fabrics. On interlock canvas, the horizontal threads actually pass through the vertical threads where they intersect, creating a firm, immovable grid. Interlock is a particularly simple and pleasant sort of canvas to use, and is especially suitable for beginners because a good quality of work can be achieved with very little experience.

All the pieces in this book have been worked in full cross stitch. The grid of 10 mesh, interlock canvas is the perfect size for this stitch when it is worked with modern 4-ply tapestry wool. If half-cross stitch or tent stitch is used instead, then canvas with smaller holes, such as 12 mesh, would be preferable as the white canvas threads can be seen through the stitches if 10 mesh is used.

Whatever canvas is chosen, sufficient should always be bought to allow at least a 2 in (5 cm) and preferably a 3 in (7.5 cm) margin around the finished area of woolwork. Before starting to stitch, many people bind the edges of their canvas with masking tape to stop them unravelling. This procedure, though not strictly necessary with interlock canvas because it does not fray easily, is advisable in order to protect clothes and to stop the wool snagging on the cut edges of the canvas.

Woolwork should always be stitched with the selvedge running up the side of the piece being worked because the shape of the completed piece of woolwork will then be squarer. If a piece is worked with the selvedge running along the top or bottom, then the shape tends to become rather elongated. This point is especially important to remember if the finished piece is destined to be part of a carpet.

Wool

All the designs in this book have been worked with Elizabeth Bradley 4-ply tapestry wool. This range of wools contains 154 colours. Most needlework designers like to use their own distinctive range of wool colours and often have their special favourites among them. The extent to which one colour reacts with another when placed next to it, is sometimes not appreciated. Some colours harmonize and enhance one another while others tend to clash. Over several years and through a process of trial and error I have evolved this range of wool for my work. Some of the wools are brightly coloured, but most are rather muted shades so that the resulting work has a rich and antique look. Since most traditional furnishing fabrics use a similar range of colours, needlework using these wools will fit into many different rooms. Before buying tapestry wool for a project it is advisable to consider the colours carefully.

The Elizabeth Bradley Wool Book, containing samples of all the wools organized onto 14 detachable cards, is invaluable for this purpose. The individual shade cards can be taken out of The Wool Book and held against furnishing fabrics, carpets, wallpaper or existing examples of woolwork. Colours can be matched and coordinated and subtle backgrounds chosen for various designs and patterns. The Wool Book is also invaluable for identifying the Elizabeth Bradley wools remaining when a kit has been completed – these may then be used to work projects from this book.

The wool used for each design in this book has been carefully chosen and, to get really satisfactory reproductions of the worked models illustrated, it is best to use exactly the same wools. In my experience, some colours from other ranges convert reasonably well but many do not and so the resulting pieces of needlework are often disappointing if other brands of wool are used.

Wool quantities

The wool quantities given in this book are for the number of yards of Elizabeth Bradley 4-ply tapestry wool that is needed to sew a design if cross stitch is used and if the work is done on 10 mesh, interlock canvas. These quantities should be approximately halved if half cross stitch or tent stitch are used instead.

All of the designs in this book are new and in many cases only one prototype of each design was worked. Consequently, the wool quantities given with each chart are only approximate. The quantities of wool used by different stitchers can vary enormously, especially in more complicated designs.

When the wool quantities for an Elizabeth Bradley kit are calculated, an extra 30 per cent of wool is added to the average of the amounts used to make the various prototypes (at least six prototypes are usually made). This allows for mistakes and unusual ways of working. Likewise, the wool quantities given in this book include an extra 30 per cent added to the wool that was used to make the prototype or prototypes, and because of this you may find that the wool quantities for each design err on the side of generosity.

Buying wool

Elizabeth Bradley wool is wound onto cards of two sizes. The large card contains 30 yds of wool and the small, 10 yds. Care should be taken not to mix wool of different types as the thickness and degree of twist of one brand of wool can vary considerably from another. Using several together can result in an unevenly textured piece of work.

The exact shade of a wool colour may vary slightly between dye lots though the differences are minimal these days and will only occasionally cause problems. However even a slight difference can result in a shadowy line across an area of background and so if a large area is being worked it is probably best to buy all the necessary wool in one batch.

Victorian cross stitch

All the designs in this book have been worked in cross stitch. Finished pieces worked in this stitch are thicker than those made with tent stitch and so they tend to be more hard wearing. Cross stitch is easy to work and as each cross forms its own small square the pattern looks particularly distinct. Pieces worked in cross stitch do not become distorted, because each stitch pulls first to the right and then to the left and so the finished needlework remains square. It is therefore unnecessary to use a frame unless you prefer to do so.

There are a number of ways of working cross stitch. The particular version shown in the diagram overleaf is one that is often found on pieces of Victorian woolwork. It is a very easy and satisfactory stitch to work although it can be somewhat extravagant with wool. The wool quantities that are given with each chart allow for the use of this cross stitch worked on 10 mesh interlock canvas. Cross stitch should always be used when making carpets because the finished piece needs to remain square. Carpets worked in tent stitch would almost certainly require extensive stretching and reshaping and however carefully this is done they always tend to creep back to being diamond- or parallelogram-shaped.

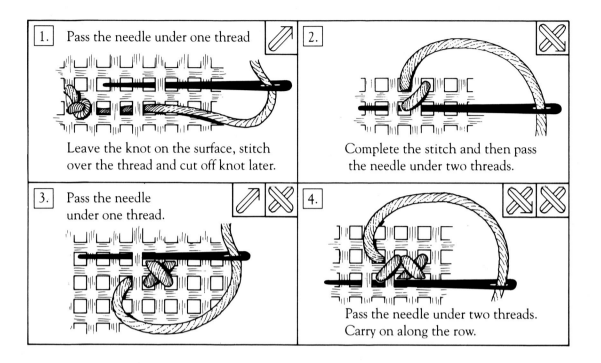

1. Pass the needle under one thread

Leave the knot on the surface, stitch over the thread and cut off knot later.

2.

Complete the stitch and then pass the needle under two threads.

3. Pass the needle under one thread.

4.

Pass the needle under two threads. Carry on along the row.

Making cross stitches

To start, leave a knot on the surface about 1 in (2.5 cms) from where you want to begin. Stitch over this strand of wool, making sure to catch it up with the stitches, then cut the knot off as you come to it.

• Pass the needle under one thread of canvas.

• Complete the stitch and then pass the needle under two threads of canvas.

• Repeat the first step, passing the needle under one thread of canvas.

• Once again pass the needle under two threads of canvas. The needle moves horizontally at all times.

Cross stitch should always be worked so that the second of the two short stitches of the cross all lie in the same direction.

Right-handed stitchers work from right to left.

Left-handed stitchers turn the diagram upside down and work from left to right.

The appearance of the finished work

The appearance of a piece of finished woolwork depends on various factors. One of these is the smoothness and regularity with which the work is done. If the lengths of wool can be persuaded to pass through the canvas without jagging, twisting and jerking then the look of the finished piece will be much smoother and more lustrous. Practice and experience help to achieve an easy and relaxed working style. The length of the strand of wool used in the needle is also important. Long lengths of thread twist more than shorter ones and can become thin and frayed by the time the end has been reached. Approximately 30 ins (75 cms) of thread seems to be a good practical length.

Another factor that affects appearance is the direction in which the lengths of wool are used. Wool has a right and a wrong way. If a length of wool is pulled gently between the fingers or lips then one direction should feel slightly smoother than the other. Work should always be done with the wool passing through the canvas in this direction, it will behave much better. If a length of thread is being troublesome then try turning it around.

The quality of a finished piece can also be affected by the tension of the stitches – the term tension means how tightly each stitch is pulled. Stitches should not be pulled tightly at all or the wool becomes stretched and thin, nor should they be so slack as to form loops. The finished piece will be smoother and even slightly larger in size if the tension is kept quite loose. Tugging at each stitch causes the piece of work to become puckered and may actually make it slightly smaller. Ideally, the same tension should be used throughout a piece; the ability to achieve this uniformity comes with practice as does an easy and personal rhythm of stitching.

Pieces of needlework that are obviously well executed tend to have very neat and tidy backs. To help achieve this, ends of wool should be cut off close to the back of the work and long loops stretching from one group of stitches to another should be avoided. If long ends and loops of more than ½in (12mm) are left at the back of a piece they become caught up with other stitches and the work can become terribly thick and matted.

Starting and finishing

To begin stitching, tie a large knot in the end of the wool. This knot will be left on the front of the work about 1in (2.5cm) in front of where the stitches will start. The first few stitches should catch up and hold the end of the wool (between the knot and the first stitch) in place at the back of the work and the knot can then be snipped off when it is reached.

To finish off, take the end of the length of wool to the back of the work and thread it through between six and ten stitches before cutting it off. Take care to finish off each strand of wool properly – if the ends of wool are not anchored down when starting and finishing they can work loose very easily making constant repairs necessary.

Correcting mistakes

It is easy, especially when tired, to make small mistakes when following a chart. Most of these mistakes can be put right quite easily by either undoing a few stitches and then re-working them or by adapting that part of the pattern slightly so that the mistake just merges in with the rest of the design.

If an area of stitches does need to be undone then it should be done with great care. Each stitch should be snipped through with a small, pointed pair of scissors and the cut ends then pulled out. When the section is re-worked, take care to anchor down any stray ends of wool with the new stitches.

If a thread of the canvas gets cut by mistake it is possible to repair it by cutting a small square of canvas from the side of the work and tacking it behind the damaged area so that the position of the holes and the mesh coincide exactly. The new stitches can be worked through the main canvas and the patch together and a practically invisible mend achieved.

Working from a chart

Contrary to what many people think, working from a chart is both straightforward and surprisingly easy once the eye has grown used to following the squared pattern. Each square on the chart represents one stitch and each stitch is worked over an intersection of a horizontal and a vertical thread of canvas. It is the threads of the canvas that should be counted, not the holes as one might think – hence the name counted thread work.

Reading a chart becomes quite simple once this principle is established and all that is then required is careful counting. Each square has been painted in a shade that is as similar as possible to that of the wool that will be used to stitch it. Some of the wool colours used in a design are very similar and so symbols have been added where necessary to help avoid confusion.

Working instructions

Where to start sewing is, to a certain extent, a matter of personal preference, as is the way in which the design is worked. Some people start in the centre of a new project, work the picture part of a design first and then fill in the background later. Others start at the top and then proceed downwards. I like to start at the bottom of a piece and work upwards because I find the stitch easier to work this way. I also like to see the pattern growing upwards from the bottom of the piece rather than downwards from the top. I tend to work the pictorial part of the design when I am feeling reasonably fresh and the background in the evening when I am tired or when I am chatting or watching television.

Some of the colours used in my designs are very similar and the small differences between them can be difficult to see in bad or artificial light, it is best to work these sections in daylight when the difference between the colours shows up more clearly. If working in daylight is not possible, then a daylight bulb is a good substitute.

A design is made up of areas of different colours, some large and some small. Aim to work as much as possible of an area or block of one colour before moving on to the next. Plan a "route" around the pattern so as to avoid having to start and finish off more than is necessary. Each row of stitches, whether long or short, should be worked from right to left (or left to right if you are left-handed). If the row is longer than seven or eight stitches, finish it off at the far end and start the next row afresh. If the gap between the end of one row of stitches and the beginning of the next is less than seven or eight stitches then a short loop can be left between them. Alternatively, to give a neater finish, the wool can be woven through the back of the stitches until the new starting point is reached.

Sometimes a colour is dotted about in small areas all over the design (a stitch here, two there and so on). It is tempting to loop from one area to another but this is bad practice unless the dots or small areas of colour are very close together. Long loops tend to get caught up and pulled tight by other stitches and this can cause the piece to become puckered and thick.

When working the background, start at the right-hand side (or left-hand side if you are left-handed) of the canvas and work all the way across to the other side. Finish off at the end of each row and start again on the right using the rest of the wool left in the needle. If each row of the background is started with a new length of wool in the needle then all the lengths will finish at approximately the same place which can cause vertical and rather unsightly lines at intervals across the width of the finished background area. It is best to work all the rows of the background from right to left because it achieves a smooth and even finish over the background area. Turning the canvas upside down at the end of each row and working the next row back the other way may seem quicker and easier but it creates a ridged effect.

Many needleworkers are absolute perfectionists. They produce magnificent work in which each stitch exactly mirrors an equivalent square on the chart, the back of such work often being as exquisite as the front. Most of us start out with this ideal in mind but fall down in the actual practice. On the whole we are content to have a completed piece of work which looks good even if it does contains a few inconsistencies.

The group of needleworkers who are likely to have the most problems are those beginners who are also absolute perfectionists, for them there is no pleasure in producing work that is not totally accurate and yet their lack of experience makes this difficult. I can only suggest that they tackle simple projects until they become more expert.

Finishing

When finished, a piece of needlework should be pressed on its reverse side through a damp cloth or with a steam iron. If the finished piece is at all out of shape then it should be stretched or blocked. To do this, dampen it and stretch it into shape, then pin it out to dry by fixing it down with carpet tacks or drawing pins onto a board making sure that the edges are straight and the corners at 90 degrees.

Cleaning

For the purposes of cleaning, it is helpful to regard woolwork as a type of thick woollen upholstery fabric which can be washed but only if absolutely necessary and with great care, using a gentle soap powder and warm water. On the whole, it is much safer to have a finished piece dry cleaned, especially if it has already been made up into a cushion. The colours of modern tapestry wool are fast and do not run, but water softens the threads of the canvas which may then fray around the edges. A finished cushion can become puckered if the woolwork and its backing shrink to different degrees.

If a piece of woolwork has been used as a cover for an upholstered stool or chair then dry cleaning is impossible. In this case, just vacuum clean the surface of the stool or chair, to remove any dust or loose dirt particles and then sponge the needlework with upholstery foam. Wool is protected from dirt by its own natural oils but extra protection can be given by spraying a freshly completed piece with a protective fluid.

Antique woolwork should never by washed by an amateur as many of the colours run and the canvas threads will have been weakened by age. Water would soften these fibres further and might even cause them to disintegrate completely. If an antique piece needs serious cleaning, it is advisable to leave the job to a professional textile restorer.

Upholstered furniture

Pieces of woolwork make excellent covers for most types of upholstered furniture. Stools and chairs are the items most usually covered, but the ambitious could try covering whole armchairs or ottomans.

Before a new needlework cover is attached to a piece of furniture, it is advisable to have the upholstery overhauled. It is well worth having this done professionally and by traditional methods because then the piece, with its new needlework cover, should last for many years without further restoration or repair.

Many classic pieces of furniture are now reproduced and their manufacturers or stockists should be able to provide templates for their covers. If such a template is not available, then the best way to determine the shape and size of a prospective chair or stool cover is to remove its original cover and use it as a pattern for the replacement. If this is not possible then all that can be done is to measure the dimensions of the seat and draw out the approximate shape on the canvas, leaving a generous margin around the edge in case of error.

Cushions

The majority of woolwork pieces stitched today are made into cushions. Backing materials suitable for such cushions are cotton velvet, watered silk, ottoman cloth, linen or fine wool, all of which are traiditional for this purpose. Most cushions are fitted with a zip which is usually inserted along the bottom or across the back. Many antique cushions were embellished with a cord sewn around the edge and a tassel at each corner. The cord and tassels should be sewn on by hand after the cushion has been made and a wide range of attractive cord and tassels are now available from department stores and specialist shops.

Cord unravels very quickly if the ends are left free and so they should be bound with thread or a small piece of adhesive tape to keep them together. Attach the cord by hand, stitching it all the way around using button thread. The cord should not be pulled tight as it is being sewn on but let it lie easy and unstretched against the edges of the cushion.

To start, poke one end of the cord into a small gap made in the seam and sew it in place. Continue sewing right around the cushion and back to the starting point. The other end of the cord should then be pushed in next to the first and the two firmly stitched in place to make as invisible a join as possible. The tassels can be attached as each corner is reached; each tassel has a loop on top and the cord should be pushed through this loop to secure the tassel.

An alternative trim would be piping made from silk fabric cut on the cross and wrapped around a length of piping cord. A small piece of needlework can be extended by using it as the centrepiece of a fabric frame made from strips of material with their corners mitred.

Framing

Pieces of Victorian woolwork were often displayed framed on the wall rather than as cushions. Mellow, golden, maple mouldings were by far the most popular type of frame in the nineteenth century and modern maple framing is still widely used around needlework pictures and samplers. Victorian pictures were normally glazed to protect them against the soot and tar from coal fires. Today, with our centrally heated houses, this is no longer necessary and so framed woolwork is often left unglazed.

Before a piece of woolwork can be framed it is essential to stretch it. In the past the work would have been tacked to a specially made wooden stretcher before being placed in the frame. Today, however, it is more usual to stretch it carefully over a piece of hardboard or card before framing.

The hardboard should be slightly smaller than the frame. Place the needlework face downwards on a table, spray lightly with water and lay the hardboard on top. Using thin string or strong twine, lace the top and bottom edges together, gradually pulling the string tighter and tighter. This should be done gently because if the string or twine is jerked tight suddenly it might break and could even tear the canvas: time is needed for the canvas to stretch to its fullest extent. When laced tight enough, repeat the process with the lacing running from one side of the piece to the other.

Once the picture is in its frame, back it with card or mounting board cut to the right shape. This can then be fastened down with panel pins or metal triangles from a mounting gun. Finally, cover the join between card and frame with gummed paper tape. It is always interesting to see pictures that have been signed and dated, it adds interest and such details are a kindness to future generations who may want to know more about a piece and the person who made it.

RIGHT: A square carpet or wall hanging made from nine central squares surrounded by the Ivy Border. They are worked on a red (B8) background. The three squares that form the bottom row of the carpet and the square on the right-hand side of the middle row, are from the Natural History Series of kits. They are Woodland, Duck Pond, Hedgerow and Meadow, and are only available in kit form.

Information

Elizabeth Bradley needlework kits

All the designs in *Needlework Animals* are new. None of them are available as kits, they all have to be worked from the charts in the book. A further selection of Elizabeth Bradley designs can be obtained in the form of full kits and a list of those available is given below. In addition, there are several animal patterns in the two previous books by the same author. Charts for The Parrot, Rabbits, Dash the Spaniel and The Tabby Cat can be found in the first book, *Decorative Victorian Needlework*, while the designs for The Blackbirds' Nest, The Robin, and The Nasturtium and Butterfly Border are featured in the second book *Needlework Antique Flowers*.

The full range of Elizabeth Bradley Needlework Kits is as follows:

The Victorian Animal Series
(16 x 16 ins [40 x 40 cms])

VA01 The Cream Cat
VA02 The King Charles Spaniel
VA03 The Cockerel
VA04 The Mother Hen
VA05 The Parrot
VA06 The Three Birds
VA07 Toby the Pug
VA08 The Contented Cat
VA09 The Spotted Dog
VA10 The Squirrel
VA11 The Lion
VA12 The Elephant

The Beasts of the Field Series
(13.3 x 20.3 ins [33.25 x 50.75 cms])

BF01 The Gloucester Old Spot Sow with
    her Piglets
BF02 The Shorthorn Ox
BF03 The Suffolk Punch and a Hound
BF04 Two Fat Suffolk Lambs

The Natural History Series
(16 x 16 ins [40 x 40 cms])

NH01 Meadow
NH02 Hedgerow
NH03 Duck Pond
NH04 Woodland

The Four Seasons - Victorian Flower Series
(16 x 16 ins [40 x 40 cms])

VF01 Spring
VF02 Summer
VF03 Autumn
VF04 Winter

A Flowered Victorian Bell Pull
(46 x 6 ins [117 x 15 cms])

The Fruits of the Earth Series
(16 x 16 ins [40 x 40 cms])

FE01 Strawberries
FE02 A Bowl of Fruit
FE03 Vegetables
FE04 A Wreath of Herbs

Decorative Victorian Needlework
(16 x 16 ins [40 x 40 cms])

VN01 A Wreath of Roses
VN02 Repeating Roses
VN03 A Posy of Violets
VN04 Patchwork Pieces

The Botanical Garden
(16 x 16 ins [40 x 40 cms])

BG01 The Crocus
BG02 The Daffodil
BG03 The Tulip
BG04 The Auricula
BG05 The Pink
BG06 The Rose
BG07 The Daisy
BG08 The Lily
BG09 The Hollyhock
BG10 The Hydrangea
BG11 The Pansy
BG12 The Cyclamen

Floribunda
(12 x 12 ins [30.5 x 30.5 cms])

FB01 Cottage Garden Favourites
FB02 A Garland of Pansies
FB03 A Victorian Posy
FB04 Clematis, Roses and Butterflies

A Taste of Elizabeth Bradley
(6 x 6 ins [15.2 x 15.2 cms])

MK01 The Spaniel Puppy
MK02 Baby Wreath
MK03 Fruit and Birds
MK04 Poppy and Butterfly

All Elizabeth Bradley kits contain the following items:

- A piece of white, interlock, Blueline canvas (10 holes to the inch) printed with the design and the wool colour code.
- A card showing a full size, finished piece on the front and a coloured chart on the back. Simple yet comprehensive instructions for working the kit are printed inside the card.
- Enough Elizabeth Bradley 4-ply tapestry wool to complete both the design and the background in Victorian cross stitch.
- A woolcard threaded with samples of the choice of background colours and numbered samples of the wools used in the design. Up to 30 colours are used in some of the kits.
- Two needles.
- A gift box containing all the above items.

The following items and services are also available from Elizabeth Bradley Designs Limited and their distributors:
- Elizabeth Bradley 4-ply tapestry wool, wound onto cards of two sizes:
Large - 30 yards and Small - 10 yards.
- A Wool Book containing samples of the full range of 154 Elizabeth Bradley wools.
- Elizabeth Bradley Blue Line Canvas, 10 mesh interlock canvas, 1m wide, available by the metre.
- Cord, Tassels and Brass Bell Pull Ends.
- The Ribbon and Bow Carpet Border Kit available in red, blue or green.
- The Books *Decorative Victorian Needlework* and *Needlework Antique Flowers* by Elizabeth Bradley.
- A Cushion Making Service.
- A Framing Service.

Elizabeth Bradley wool

All Elizabeth Bradley needlework patterns whether in kit form or printed as charts in a book are designed to be worked with Elizaeth Bradley wools.

Obtaining Elizabeth Bradley products

For details of how to obtain the full range of kits, accessories and services in the United Kingdom and Overseas please contact:

Elizabeth Bradley Designs Limited
1 West End
Beaumaris
Anglesey
N Wales
LL58 8BD
Tel: 01248 811055
Fax: 01248 811118
e-mail: ebd@elizabethbradley.co.uk

US customers may order by telephoning:
Toll Free: 1 (800) 635 0974

Conversion Chart

The projects shown in this book have been designed for and worked with Elizabeth Bradley wools. Alternative wools will not yield the same results as colours and textures will differ. Although the alternatives listed here are correct at the time of publication, manufacturers' ranges change periodically and you should check availability with your local stockist. See page 165 for details of how to order Elizabeth Bradley wools.

Numbers in brackets = nearest available equivalent colour

Elizabeth Bradley wools	DMC wools
A1	7120
A2	7950
A3	7761
A4	7354
A5	7196
A6	7147
A7	7449
A8	7218
A9	7463
A10	7465
A11	7165
B1	7451
B2	7543
B3	7164
B4	7123
B5	7124
B6	7146
B7	7178
B8	7447
B9	7125
B10	7920
B11	7127
C1	7492
C2	7503
C3	7472
C4	(7725)
C5	7505
C6	7780
C7	7767
C8	7444
C9	7175
C10	7875
C11	7700
D1	7420
D2	7470
D3	(7504)
D4	(7727)
D5	7473
D6	(7484)
D7	(7785)
D8	7677
D9	(7485)
D10	7487
D11	7490
E1	(7461)
E2	7724
E3	7463
E4	7494
E5	7421
E6	7508
E7	7845
E8	7457
E9	7459
E10	7479
E11	7458
F1	blanc
F2	blanc
F3	ecru
F4	7450
F5	7411
F6	7511
F7	7413
F8	7524
F9	7514
F10	7488
F11	7526
G1	7520
G2	7519
G3	(7465)
G4	(7465)
G5	7518
G6	7467
G7	7938
G8	7468
G9	7515
G10	7419
G11	noir
H1	7509
H2	7390
H3	(7415)
H4	7391
H5	7515
H6	7510
H7	7282
H8	7618
H9	(7273)
H10	7626
H11	7622
I1	7583
I2	(7353)
I3	7493
I4	7363
I5	7426
I6	(7362)
I7	7364
I8	7355
I9	(7355)
I10	7391
I11	7425
J1	7371
J2	(7422)
J3	7424
J4	(7384)
J5	7376
J6	(7364)
J7	(7367)
J8	7890
J9	7379
J10	7770
J11	7988
K1	7321
K2	7331
K3	7392
K4	7394
K5	7396
K6	7398
K7	7398
K8	7704
K9	7703
K10	7406
K11	7408
L1	7322
L2	7692
L3	7927
L4	7326
L5	7327
L6	7329
L7	7429
L8	7292
L9	7293
L10	7592
L11	7297
M1	7304
M2	7650
M3	7306
M4	7587
M5	7568
M6	7284
M7	7799
M8	7308
M9	7590
M10	(7245)
M11	(7791)
N1	7232
N2	(7234)
N3	7236
N4	7238
N5	7213
N6	7223
N7	7226
N8	7115
N9	7264
N10	(7895)
N11	(7257)

Acknowledgments

My grateful thanks to the needlewomen and men who stitched the prototypes for this book with such skill and patience:

Janet Blow for the Tawny Owl.

Patricia Bradley for a Carpet Python and two lengths of Ivy Leaf Border.

Mrs Carciero for three letters of the Animal Alphabet.

Tasha Davies for a Pointer, a Marmalade Cat, two lengths of Ivy Leaf Border, a Shell Wreath and for helping with the Animal Atlas carpet.

Vicky Evans for a Mackerel line.

Mrs Fairhead for a Vegetable Garden and a Marmalade Cat.

Sharon Granton for a Moorland, three lengths of Ivy Leaf Border and the long Parrot Chain.

Sandy Hatenboer for a Moorland.

Gill Hughes for four letters of the Animal Alphabet and two lengths of Ivy Leaf Border.

Moira Hughes for a River Bank.

Gillian Jones for a Hound and two lengths of Ivy Leaf Border.

Gerrie Kostick for a letter of the Animal Alphabet and the Animal Atlas carpet.

Joanne Mitchell for a Rockpool.

Mrs G Lamb for a Butterflies.

Mr D Lewis for a Troutstream, two Mackerel and two lengths of Ivy Leaf Border.

Gaynor Owen for a length of Ivy Leaf Border.

Lynda Owen for a letter of the Animal Atlas, a Troutstream, two Mackerel and two lengths of Ivy Leaf Border.

Lynn Page for a Butterfly strip.

Mr Puryer for a letter of the Animal Alphabet and a Tiger.

Mrs Puryer for four letters of the Animal Alphabet, a Harvest Field, two Mackerel, a Butter-fly strip and two lengths of Ivy Leaf Border.

Mrs Reston for a Carpet Python and two lengths of Ivy Leaf Border.

Carys Roberts for five letters of the Animal Alphabet, a Rockpool and a Vegetable Garden.

Irene Roberts for the Animal Alphabet 1-9 cushion and the Pig Pillow.

Jane Roberts for a River Bank and a Rockpool.

Jan Sandham for finishing the Happy Birthday rug and joining the nine panel Natural History carpet.

Helen Snook for the short Parrot Chain.

Mairwen Strom for a Troutstream.

Sharon Timmis for the Mackerel Bell Pull.

Gordon Tucker for four letters of the Animal Alphabet, a Chickens and the Happy Birthday rug which he completed with the help of Joyce Tucker.

Joyce Tucker for two letters of the Animal Alphabet and the Whale Bath Mat.

Anthea Wells for four letters of the Animal alphabet, a Harvest Field, the Fox Family Rug and the Animal Alphabet carpet.

Maurice Wells for two letters of the Animal Alphabet and for joining the six panel Natural History carpet with the help of Anthea Wells.

Angela Williams for four letters of the Animal Alphabet, two lengths of the Ivy Leaf Border and the 10 yrs old cushion.

Linda Williams for cushion making.

Jennifer Windows for two lengths of Ivy Leaf Border and a Shell Wreath.

The publishers also wish to thank the following:

Pili Pallas, Penmynydd, Anglesey, for giving me specimens of butterflies that had been reared in their butterfly houses for the photograph on pages 24-5.

Philippa Armstrong for the coral on pages 40-1.

Dorothy Dickie for the shells on pages 40-1.

John Butterfield for lending shells, coral, crabs and many other interesting bits and pieces for the photograph on pages 40-1.

RAF Valley, 74th Tiger Squadron for the loan of their tiger skin on pages 54-5.

Snowdonia Taxidermy Studios for supplying some small animals on pages 138-9.

Index